BEGINNER'S GUIDE TO RAISING CHICKENS FOR EGGS, MEAT, AND JOY

HOW TO SELECT THE PERFECT BREED, CONSTRUCT THE IDEAL COOP, REDUCE COSTS, AND ENSURE A HEALTHY FLOCK

CHARLOTTE WALSH

CONTENTS

INTRODUCTION

I had almost three acres of land in Beverly Hills. And I had a big atrium of chickens because I love that feeling of being in the country and living from the soil.

— EARTHA KITT

It was the middle of a busy week in my monotonous, routine job. I was surrounded by heaps of papers, scattered stationary items, and other individuals like myself typing away at their desktops. Although my fingers moved mechanically but perfectly from one letter to the next across the keyboard, and my eyes remained fixed on the screen in front of me in unbroken concentration, my mind was in its own space, far from the moment of reality. It was wandering aimlessly in a bid to find a solution to the deep sense of frustration that I felt in those days. I had a lucrative job, a decent home, and a fairly promising future ahead of me, yet I felt unfulfilled. The unintended change of the computer screen that was in front of me brought to the fore an image that helped me transform my suppressed aspirations into the reality of my existence. Before me was a picturesque field with a flock of chickens on one side and a freshwater body on the other. The space in between was covered in lush, green vegetation, and a little home on the north end of the property created the image of a complete and satisfied life. I came to the realization that the urban way of existence that was built on mutual dependence was not for me. I wanted to pursue an independent, organic, and self-sufficient life. I knew that the ambition, if realized, would help me build a tranquil and satisfactory world for myself, but the path to bring this dream to fruition was arduous. I lived in a city and I didn't have the space that I thought was required to raise poultry. Would I have enough resources to purchase land in the remote interiors of the rural regions as well as establish the infrastructure that would be required to raise the birds? Although I came from a farming background, I didn't have specific knowledge with respect to managing chickens, maintaining them in good health, and harvesting the produce. The scientific aspect of knowing which breed was correct for the requirements of my family as well as for the geographical location in which I lived was another question that made the thought of owning a self-sufficient farm seem over-whelming. I had no information on the legal frame-work for maintaining a poultry farm in America, and I feared that with my personal commitments and work-related responsibilities, I would not be able to dedicate the time and care that the fragile birds would need to thrive in good health. Despite these inhibitions, I took the plunge, and the rewarding feeling that I discovered after the attempt is beyond expression. The pride and pleasure that I derive from living a self-sufficient, simple, but fulfilling life inspires me to share my experiences with others. This book will not only help you provide for your family's food necessities, but it will also make it possible for you to turn into an entrepreneur by selling your organic produce, if you so desire. Pursuing a sustainable life in this way will aid you in your objective of living with self-sufficiency, fulfillment, and monetary independence.

The concept of self-sufficiency has gained traction in recent times. Many people dream of becoming independent with respect to meeting their basic needs for existence. With the growing stress that is associated with a standard desk job in an urban setting, the idea of owning a large farm with organic produce and a little family retreat has become all the more appealing. The term sustenance, however, has a different meaning for different people. For example, you may want to become self-sufficient to be able to consume fresh food from your own field or backyard on an everyday basis, or you may want to store the nutritious summer produce for the tough winter months. Some individuals choose self-sufficiency to attain financial stability without having to work a fixed 9-to-5 job, while many others view the prospect of sustenance as an opportunity to regain their sense of fulfillment by liberating them-selves from debt and the sometimes unnecessary shenanigans of city life. Whatever your motivation is behind wanting to cultivate your own food from your own land, the practice will certainly yield benefits that will make your life more rewarding and satisfying. The obvious advantage of maintaining self-sustenance is that you will be able to produce and meet the everyday food requirements of your family. What's more, you will no longer have to depend on grocery stores or local markets for your fresh food needs. While these avenues may appear convenient and easy, growing vegetables and/or raising poultry yourself can have tremendous positives in unforeseen circumstances. For example, think just how simple life could have been if you had your own natural source of food during the global pandemic. Moreover, when you work toward self-sufficiency, you are likely to move away from bingeing on burgers or fries. Instead, you will be drawn toward consuming the healthier alternatives like organic fruits or fresh eggs from your farm. This will improve your physical well-being immensely. Living close to nature creates a sense of fulfillment that can be matched by no other urban accomplishment. While these outcomes may seem inviting, the path to bringing these aspirations to fruition can be daunting, particularly if you are new to farming. Leaving behind your established world in a town or city and moving to the countryside in search of a tranquil existence is a major transformation that may necessitate significant levels of sacrifice and adjustments on your part. It will be reassuring to know in this context that self-sustenance can begin from where you are currently. You could start by growing herbs or other greens on the balcony of your apartment, or even in more confined indoor spaces like the basement or a rarely used corner of your home. To live entirely on your produce, however, you will likely need to invest in land, approximately between three to five acres in size, depending on whether you aspire to use it to grow vegetables or maintain a flock. The ideal start to accomplish your sustenance goals is to alter your lifestyle—a minimalistic approach to everyday activities with a modest desire for materialistic possessions is important in order to sustain your goals over a period of time. Some of the steps that you could take in this direction include reducing avoidable expenses, purchasing necessities at discounted rates, selling the articles that you no longer use, downsizing your home, paying off your debts, embracing environmentally friendly processes like using recycled clothing, and so on. Stocking up your pantry with items that are in season or are being sold at reduced prices can help you sustain through the tough months with relative ease. Growing your own fruits, vegetables, herbs, and spices, or raising your own source of meat through poultry, is a well-known path to attaining the objective of living completely off the land. When you own a farm, you will not only be able to satisfy the food requirements of your household, but you will also be able to become an entrepreneur in your own capacity. Selling your organic produce at rural markets or through online mediums is an excellent way to earn useful sums of money to supplement your sustenance. Agricultural land also has the opportunity to capitalize on secondary sources of business income. For example, you could make money by opening up your farm to students or curious tourists for learning or recreational visits, or you could sublet parts of your land on a temporary basis. Thus, adopting a mindful approach to managing expenses, food consumption, storage, and utilizing your produce from the land can help you remain self-sufficient for as long as you desire.

When I think of self-sufficiency, one of the first things that comes to mind is a poultry farm. Nurturing chickens to meet your self-sufficiency goals is a viable option for a number of reasons. The birds are relatively easy to manage, and if you understand the science behind choosing the type of breed and the number that is correct for your personal needs and entrepreneurial aspirations, the option can prove to be a highly cost-effective one. Chickens also help with improving the biological health of your farm as they create natural fertilizers through their excrement. They also help in optimum waste management for they can feed on a diverse range of organic and inorganic debris. The succeeding pages of this publication will delve deeper into the subject of using chickens as your food source as well as your income medium. Without further ado, dearest readers, I urge you to turn the page and take your first step toward self-satisfaction, self-fulfillment, and self-sustenance.

1

FINDING YOUR SPRING CHICKEN

When I abandoned my city life, I not only discovered a sense of fulfillment in owning my own poultry farm, but I came to realize the many advantages that the practice had for my overall well-being. A journey that began with bringing home six fragile little hens evolved into a tale of self-sustenance through poultry for over two decades because of these innumerable benefits. All my fears and apprehensions about my abilities with respect to raising a flock of chickens gradually faded away when I finally took the plunge and trusted myself. Once I erected a coop and guided my flock into it, I discovered the birds required little effort on my part for their maintenance. Unlike some of my previous pets, they did not need morning walks or constant engagement attempts. Instead, as the naturally social creatures interacted with one another, they provided never-ending entertainment and a source of happy distraction for my family. All of a sudden, I began to feel like an accomplished chef because the delicacies that I prepared using the farm produce not only felt fresh, but they also tasted better than when I previously cooked with industrial meat and eggs. I quickly understood the reason for the difference in quality between organic and commercially available perishables was the environment in which the birds were raised, as well as the nature of the feed that was given to them for their nourishment. As the owner of a poultry farm, I was in complete control of the diet of my chickens, and this reflected unambiguously in the kind of produce that I was able to generate from my flock. Besides providing a sustainable food source for my family, the birds helped keep my land free of disease-carrying bugs and pests. When they were allowed to scour the field freely throughout the day, the chickens displayed the diverse nature of their diets as they ate everything from grasshoppers and mosquitoes to fruit peels and cooked food like rice and pasta. As a new landowner, I was initially agitated by the quantity of natural waste that chickens produced on a daily basis. This was, however, only until I learned of the immense benefits of using their poop as a non-chemical fertilizer for my field. This positively impacted the volume and quality of fresh produce like vegetables and other crops on my land. Our physical well-being improved greatly as a result, as it is even scientifically proven that organic vegetables and eggs of non-industrial chickens have a higher nutritional content than those produced commercially. The eggs of chickens that are raised in a free environment are a richer source of vitamin E and omega-3 fatty acids, both of which are essential components for human health. While home raised chickens provide immense benefits, all chickens and eggs are not created equal. Let's dive deeper into discovering the chicken breed that will be best suited for you and your family.

GETTING ACQUAINTED WITH THE MANY CHICKEN BREEDS

There are a multitude of varieties of chickens, and to be able to decide on which breed might be perfect for you, it's important to become aware of these distinct types. A comprehensive list of the classification of chickens based on their specific features can be found at the end of this book in the appendix section. Some of the most common variants of roosters and hens, though, are discussed below.

Brown Layers

Australorp: Native to Australia, this breed of chicken is known for its high volume of egg production. The small, light brown eggs are nutritious and delicious, and the hens of the breed will lay them without requiring much human interference.

Barnvelder: Having originated in the Netherlands, these birds are universally well-known for their colorful feathers and beautiful overall appearance. They rarely grow into large sized creatures and their hens are most fertile during the winter months.

Bielefelder: This breed is the result of a purposeful biological mating of two different species of the bird. This chicken variant is a hybrid, which means that it can be used to meet both your meat and egg requirements. They produce uniquely colored and large-sized eggs consistently throughout the year. As they are friendly with humans, this breed also makes excellent pets.

Black / Red Star: With this chicken variety, you will be able to tell apart a male from a female newborn chick with relative ease. They produce eggs, which can vary greatly in color, all year.

Brahma: Arguably the largest variety of the bird in terms of size, this breed is appreciated for its meat and eggs in equal measure. They are extremely fertile between the end of fall and the onset of spring. They are best suited for regions that do not experience extremely high temperatures.

Buckeye: This sprightly, red-colored breed was created by the intentional crossing of two established species types by an American woman in the 20th century. They can easily thrive in any environment, and they can be used both for their eggs and for their meat.

Chantecler: Ideal for Canadian weather conditions, the Chantecler produces light brown-colored eggs year-round. The birds are most fertile when they're allowed to wander about the farm freely. Confining them to small spaces will inversely affect the quality of their produce.

Delaware: This American chicken breed was developed in 1940. The bird grows large enough to be used for its meat. It regularly produces brown-colored eggs across all seasons.

Java: Another American breed, this variety of chicken has been consumed since the 19th century. The variant comes in different colors, and each of those types stands out for the unique shade of its feathers.

Jersey Giant: As can be implied from the name, this breed was developed in New Jersey, and these birds are extremely large in size. They consistently lay high-quality eggs throughout the year. A production volume of anywhere between 200 and 250 eggs annually is a reasonable expectation for this variety.

Maran: A French breed, this variety is also relatively well-known for its capacity to produce anywhere between 150 and 200 eggs in one year. Owing to their distinctly dark brown color, the eggs of a Maran are easy to identify when buying from a market or grocery store.

Naked Neck: This variety of chicken is so named because it is completely devoid of feathers in the neck region of its physical structure. This means that the bird has greater environmental exposure through its skin, and this also makes it easy to use the little creature for meat. This variant of chicken is highly disease-resistant, and its free-ranging personality makes it ideal for backyard breeding.

Orpington: This breed is well appreciated for its brown eggs as well as its white meat. These chickens are known for being "city dwellers" because they do well in limited spaces. They are friendly and non-aggressive so they get on well with other chickens in your coop. Avoid them if you live in a high temperature environ-ment, however, they do fantastic in the coldest of weathers due to their extra feathers.

Plymouth Rock: Developed in the mid-1800s, the Plymouth Rock was the most popular chicken variety in American households until the middle of the 20th century. They are an excellent meat source and lay eggs year-round. Their social and adaptable personalities make them ideal for farm breeding. Overall they are a healthy, sturdy breed and can live up to 10-12 years when properly cared for.

Rhode Island Red: Perhaps the breed that demands the least out of a landowner, this chicken variant can be a convenient choice for those creating or managing a poultry farm for the first time. They can be used for their meat as well as for their eggs.

Speckled Ranger: A chicken variant known for its steady egg production all year, the Speckled Ranger is easy to raise and maintain. The birds are not aggressive, and they are excellent at consuming farm and kitchen waste.

Sussex: This is an ancient British breed that is widely used for its rich meat. The birds tend to grow very large with even a small amount of feed. Their egg production is reasonably consistent across seasons.

Welsummer: Distinctly known for their large, dark brown eggs, this breed is easy to raise because the birds are friendly and responsive to human efforts.

Wyandotte: This breed is on neither end of the spectrum when it comes to the volume of perineal egg production. They lay eggs moderately across most seasons, but they are at their most fertile during the cold winter months. They come in a variety of hues, and they thrive well in and around upstate New York and the Ontario region of Canada.

Colored Layers

Araucana: A highly uncommon variant of the bird, the Araucana was first discovered in Chile, South America. Owing to their complex biological chemistry, not many Araucana chicks manage to mature into roosters or hens. Therefore, maintaining a flock of chickens that belong exclusively to this breed may not be plausible in the long-run.

Ameraucana: This white-skinned chicken breed is fairly uncommon, and it is not possible to find them in every local store across the United States. These birds are descendants of the Araucana chicken variant, and they are particularly well-known for their ability to lay over 200 light blue-colored eggs in one calendar year.

Cream Legbar: A breed native to the United Kingdom, the Legbar is easy to raise and maintain on a farm. Hens lay eggs consistently all year and they can either be light green or blue in color. They don't do well in confinement so avoid this breed if you're limited in space.

Easter Egger: This term is not specific to a particular breed of chicken, but rather it is used to refer to any bird that has a biological mutation to produce blue-colored eggs. It is, however, not necessary that both the hen and the rooster carry this genetic coding, and therefore, it is possible that your Easter Egger produces eggs that range in color from a dusty brown to a pastel blue. Due to the Egger's capacity to produce a large volume of eggs, it makes for a useful addition to your backyard flock.

Isbar: These birds are well suited to be used as pets and also as an egg source for your family, but not meat. They lay eggs, usually in shades of green, across all seasons. Their intelligence, alertness, and foraging capabilities make them fit for a life on the farm.

Olive Egger: Another member of the green egg-laying group, the Olive Egger is a good choice for inexperienced farm owners. Their adaptability creates an opportunity for learning on an everyday basis as they can be experimented with. They are great egg layers and can be raised for meat as well.

Whiting True Blue: As can be implied from the title, this breed of chicken consistently produces blue eggs across the seasons. The eggs can be medium in size and larger as the bird matures.

White Layers

55 Flowery Hen: This breed of chicken, which produces eggs in volumes that suit commercial supply, is a native of Sweden. Its large, cream-colored eggs can be used to satisfy your family's food requirements as well as to make useful income from the sale of the fresh produce.

Ancona: The hens of this breed lay large white eggs consistently throughout all seasons. They are well suited to a life on the farm because of their social personality and innate ability to sense predators.

Andalusian: Another variety of chicken that lays white eggs, the Andalusian matures into a medium-sized bird of either blue, cream, or black color. Its physical anatomy makes it ideal for regions with warm weather. Native to Spain, the hens of this breed easily lay about 150 eggs in one year.

Brakel: A white layer variety that was first developed in Europe in the 19th century, the Brakel is widely used for its produce all across the continent, even still today. The birds, which are an attractive gold or silver color, were primitively raised on farms, and therefore they will make for an ideal addition to your backyard flock.

Cinnamon Queen: This breed of chicken is renowned for its egg-laying capacity. The hens begin to lay at a younger age when compared to most chicken varieties, and with about 300 brown eggs each year, the Cinnamon Queens are without doubt one of the most fertile breeds in the species.

Friesan: The breed is commonly used for the small white eggs that its hens produce across all seasons. A native of the Dutch northern countryside, Friesans are small birds that enjoy flying about in the wild. Although the volume of their egg production is not as high as some of the other breeds, they nevertheless make useful additions to your backyard flock.

Gournay: These birds find their origin in the Normandy region of France. They have a moderate capacity to lay eggs, but their well-developed physical structure makes them suitable for meat consumption. The birds tend to thrive well even in confined spaces, and therefore, you could consider opting for this breed if you only have a small place to raise poultry.

Hamburg: Another Dutch variant, the Hamburg is an ideal choice for a poultry farm because of its eager personality. These birds are excellent at foraging, and they have a keen eye for predators. Although they easily lay about 200 white eggs each year, the feature of their fertility that distinguishes them from the other breeds is their ability to produce eggs until the final years of their existence.

Holland: The different chicken varieties either lay eggs, function as a source of meat, or both. The dual-purpose breeds, that is, those that produce both eggs and meat, generally lay brown or other colored eggs. The Holland is perhaps the only chicken variant that functions as a meat source and lays large, white eggs. Therefore, if you choose to introduce the Holland into your flock of roosters and hens, you can be assured of a supply of premium white eggs and quality meat all through the year.

Leghorn: This breed is renowned for its white, high-quality eggs. The hens lay consistently almost everyday across all seasons. The birds are extremely social and friendly with humans. They make excellent farm pets.

Minorca: Well-known for their large, white eggs, the birds of this breed are best suited to hot weather conditions.

Bantams

Barbu D'Uccle: The breed was first developed in Belgium. These birds are active and highly adaptive. They can be raised even in small or confined spaces, however, their eggs are small in size and off-white in color.

Belgian Antwerp D'Anvers: Found in a host of colors in and around Belgium, these birds are excellent for meat because of their well-developed bodies. A poultry farm with large open spaces is ideal for these birds to thrive in good health.

Booted Bantam: If your goal behind maintaining a flock of chickens is to have friendly pets that you can lean on during rough times, then this breed is perfect for you. Their calm personality means that they are easy to tame, and their beautiful feathers make them a treat to watch. However, they are often referred to as "show birds" because they are used more for their beauty rather than their ability to produce eggs.

Chabo: This variety of bird tends to be very large in size. Since they are heavy bodied, they can be used for meat. They are fairly adaptable and they do just as well in a backyard or a garden as on a farm.

Dutch Bantam: These light, free-flying birds lay about 160 small eggs each year. They were developed in the Netherlands in the 19th century, but they are popular all across the globe today.

Nankin: This breed is well suited to being raised in small spaces, as the birds have a natural tendency to cling together as a flock. They are also small in size and easy to manage because of their tranquil personalities. They lay eggs consistently year-round.

Pekin Bantam: These chicken varieties make excellent pets as they can be tamed and held in confined spaces. Egg production from the breed is limited, and you may not be able to meet the requirements of your entire family with this variety of chicken alone.

Rosecomb Bantam: Native to the United Kingdom, this breed of Bantam is predominantly raised for its spectacular appearance. These birds are large in size and are usually either black, white, or blue. The hens lay a mere 50 eggs each year, and their meat is not commonly preferred either. As a new landowner, you may not be able to tame this variety of chicken, for the breed is reclusive and often insensitive to human effort. Therefore, these birds are only raised for showcasing in exhibits.

Scots Dumpy: This is a Scottish breed that has been raised for over 700 years. They are well suited to a life on the farm and they produce a large volume of eggs across all seasons.

Sebright: Known for both their meat and eggs, this breed is also excellent to raise as pets. They have a delightful appearance with gold and silver plumage and their adaptable nature makes them easy to manage.

Serama: This breed originated in Malaysia only recently. The birds are small in size and they thrive well as pets. Small in stature, they also produce very small eggs. Four of a Serama's eggs equate to one average sized egg. So, while they produce 200-250 eggs per year, it may not be the best option due to the small egg variety.

Barbeque Special

There are a few varieties of chicken that are well suited to being turned into classic dinner delicacies. The Barbezieux, a French variety, is one such meat. The birds are large in size, similar to the European Basque, and this makes them ideal for meat production. The hens of both these variants lay eggs moderately, but they are predominantly preferred for the preparation of barbeque recipes. The French Bresse is perhaps the most popular breed when it comes to farm-to-table delicacies. The raising of these birds is restricted to a certain geographical region in the country of its origin, and hence you may not be able to add the variant to your backyard flock. An English breed, the Cornish, also serves well to meet the food requirements of small households. It, along with the Gallina di Saluzzo from Italy is another universal favorite for dinner time treats. Other varieties of chicken that serve the dual purpose of laying eggs and producing meat include Gournay,

Ixworth, Lyonnaise, New Hampshire, and Norfolk Grey. The German Vorwerk is yet another variant that is known for its high-quality and flavorful white meat. The Redcap and the Red Shaver are also barbeque specialties, but they are equally preferred for their large colored eggs.

Crested Breeds

Crested chickens' defining characteristic is tufted feathers that stand up tall on their head. A native of Switzerland, the Appenzeller is a breed of small birds that is classically representative of this variant. Along with the Dutch Brabanter, this breed is popular for their moderate volume of egg production as well as their suitability to serve as pets. The Crevecoeur and the Houdan are both French varieties of crested chickens. The former has remained confined to the country of its origin for its meat, while the latter has been universally appreciated for its flavor on the table. The Polish is a European breed that is well known for its distinctly colored, large eggs. The Sultan from Turkey is another popular crested breed that is often used for its meat.

Ornamental Breeds

The Cochin, the Frizzle, the Malay, the Old English Game, and the Silkies are the breeds that are most commonly raised for purposes other than their meat or egg production. All of these birds are generally large in size and spectacular in appearance. Their feathers, which are either uniquely curled, exquisitely shaded, or strikingly glossy, set them apart from the other breeds in their species.

Rare Breeds

There are a number of chicken varieties that have small populations. Many of these birds are on the verge of extinction, and if you intend to raise a flock of extremely unique and hard-to-find chicks, you could consider introducing some of these into your backyard flock: Altsteirer, Brussbar, Kalifornia Grey, Catalana, Dampierre, Deathlayer, Dorking, Iowa Blue, Langshan, Marsh Daisy, Norwegian Jeahorn, Orloff, Orust, Pavlovskaya, Penedesenca, Pita Pinta Asturiana, Rhodebar, Thuringian, and Twentse. All of these varieties are useful in one aspect or another. They can either be used for poultry production, meat production, or both. Many more also thrive as pets, and others are simply raised for their striking physical appearance. A number of these rare birds had nearly been wiped out of existence at some point in the past until they were successfully revived by enthusiastic poultry keepers. They, however, still exist in very small numbers, and their populations are restricted to certain parts of the globe alone. Many of these birds never gained popularity outside the country of their origin, and several more were abandoned because of their inability to provide meat or eggs at a volume that was necessary for commercial supply. Unforeseen events such as the First World War and Second World War also played a part in propelling these rare creatures to the verge of extinction. A few of these varieties were never given legal recognition by the poultry associations in the United States, and this also contributed to their decline. Not many of these birds currently live beyond small or medium-sized flocks, and you may have to make considerable efforts to locate and introduce one of these rare birds into your backyard.

Unusual Breeds

There are a few chicken varieties that are different from the standard image of the bird in one way or another. The Ayan Cemani, for example, is unusual because of its dark color, which radiates into its internal structure as much as its exterior body. Even the blood of the bird bears a hue of black, and this makes the variety extremely uncommon. The feathers of the Campine rooster, which resemble those of a hen, make this Belgian breed different from the rest. The Cubalaya chicken from South America is unique for its animated expressions and queer physical appearance, with a feathery tail and an elongated body. Another chicken breed that is famous for its upright external structure with a long and stiff tail is the Fayoumi from Egypt. Two other French breeds, the Faverolles and La Fleche, are categorized as unusual because of their rounded bodies and peculiar feather arrangements. The only breed of chicken that has attained the recognition of a monument is the Onagadori from Japan. The birds are queer little creatures that can have tails over 25 feet long. Inspired by the splendor of the Onagadori, a similar breed was attempted in continental Europe. It came to be known as Phoenix, and these birds resemble their Japanese ancestors in terms of their long, slender tales. Another Asian chicken breed, the Shamo, was introduced into western culture merely for its attractive appearance. The birds are worthy of being displayed in an ornamental capacity, but their eggs and meat are seldom consumed. All of these unusual chicken breeds can be raised on a farm or in a backyard. They can be used either for their eggs, meat, or simply as pets. With their unusual features, these birds are sure to add excitement to your chicken flock.

SELECTING THE RIGHT BREED FOR YOU

Now that you are familiar with some of the different chicken varieties that are commonly raised on family farms or backyards, it's important to choose the breed that suits your individual circumstances. This may seem daunting at first, as you are likely to encounter a large array of chicken varieties when you visit your local seller. Therefore, it is important to invest some thought into the type of birds that you want to bring home before you make that all-important purchase. Selecting the breed that is ideal for your needs and circumstances will help you build a meaningful life around the little creatures. On the contrary, if you select a breed without forethought, you may fail as a poultry landowner, and your aspiration of leading a self-sufficient life may never be accomplished. Some of the points that you must keep in mind while choosing chickens are as follows.

Objective

The primary step in choosing a chicken breed is to define the purpose behind owning them in the first place. Do you want to have a consistent supply of fresh eggs? Or are you intrigued by the prospect of consuming meat from the chickens you raise? Or do you aspire to use the bird for both its eggs and meat? The answers to these questions will serve as a guide for which breed might be perfect for you. If you want to become self-sufficient in terms of the food requirements of your household, the size of your family and their individual preferences will also dictate the kind of birds that will be appropriate for your flock. You could also have the motivation to raise chickens simply as pets or as useful distractions for your children. Sometimes, having a basket full of colorful eggs serves as inspiration to maintain a flock. You may also be one of those enthusiastic poultry collectors who likes to have a flock of fancy and rare birds in their garden or backyard. Defining the purpose behind raising poultry can help immensely in narrowing down the list of possible breeds that you could bring home.

Geographic Location

The next step in selecting the right chicken breed for your farm or backyard is to evaluate the climatic conditions that prevail in the region where you reside. While chickens are highly adaptive birds and do well in most places, some are innately better suited to warmer climates, while others thrive in cooler regions. By applying this parameter, you will be able to short-list the specific breeds that meet your objective and the area in which you live.

Space

This is a crucial consideration when it comes to choosing chicken breeds. Some varieties are free rangers, while others do just fine in confinement. Based on whether you intend to raise the birds in your backyard or on a large parcel of land in the countryside, you will need to select the breeds that suit your space limitations. Hens and roosters are housed in a shelter known as a coop, and the amount of space you have will directly determine the number of birds that you can bring home and maintain. The larger the coop, the happier the flock. Certain breeds are extremely social and prefer larger groups, while others exist happily in relatively small flocks. In short, the amount of space you have will determine your coop size, and this will in turn affect your choice of breed.

Nature

The personality of the birds is another important factor to consider while choosing your breed. Some varieties are docile and easy to tame. Some enjoy human interaction, while others prefer to stay aloof. The type of breed you select will depend on your objective for adopting the birds as well as your ability to manage the flock. If you are new to farming, it is best to select breeds that require less maintenance and are inherently social.

Other Factors

Your personal commitment in terms of your employment and family responsibilities will also determine the type of chicken that might be right for you. If you are managing a poultry farm as a side hustle or if you travel frequently, you may be better off choosing those breeds that do well without requiring much effort from your end. Assessing the food requirements of your family and appropriately choosing the breeds that have a laying capacity and frequency that can match them, is also important. As someone new to poultry farming, it is ideal to select the breeds that are better at sensing predators and are more disease-resistant. In this way, you will be able to save yourself the trouble of finding the birds that go missing, of looking after a sick flock, and of consuming the produce of infected chickens. The availability of breeds that match your requirements is yet another vital aspect of choosing the right flock. Selecting indigenous varieties is beneficial because it provides a sense of certainty about the breed's ability to survive on your farm or in your garden. While it's true that you are the best judge of the type of chicken that will be perfect for your self-sufficiency goals, seeking the advice of neighbors or friends who may have experience managing birds in your geographical area can also help with making the right choice. The most crucial factor in selecting one or more varieties of chicken, however, is your individual preference. Follow your desires and bring home the breed that you believe can help you live off the land.

When Is the Right Time to Buy Your Chickens?

Baby chicks are sold commercially all year, so you can practically purchase them at any time. There is, however, a certain part of the year that is considered ideal. Beginning from the last week of March (or mid-April in cooler regions) until June are not only the best months to purchase these little creatures but also to hatch young offspring. This is because the climatic conditions during these months are neither too hot nor too cold for the baby chicks. Since the days are longer in the spring and early summer than in the fall or winter, natural light, which is essential for the development of the chickens, will not be a challenge during that time. The birds will be able to wander about the fields comfortably without facing the risk of contracting cold-weather-related infections. At the six-week mark, when your chicks should be ready to move out of their brooder and settle into a larger coop, May or June provide ideal climatic conditions for the young birds to mature into healthy roosters or hens. Transportation facilities, in the event that you ordered your chicks online, function smoothly during the warmer months, and the possibility of delays due to snow storms or of losing the birds because of very low temperatures is eliminated when you make your purchase during the spring season. Moreover, chicks hatched in April or May will grow sufficiently by the time winter arrives, which will prevent premature deaths in your flock. From the point of view of cost effectiveness, the spring season is also ideal for making chicken purchases. The demand for the meat of the bird is high during the winter months, that is, around Thanksgiving and Christmas, and this generally causes the prices to inflate, coupled with a drop in supply of rich varieties. Additionally, many variants of the species tend to be most fertile during the spring months, so you can expect to make a high-quality purchase during that time. Therefore, I recommend that you begin your journey toward self-sufficiency by getting your hands on the spring chicken of your preferred breed.

WHERE TO BUY YOUR CHICKENS?

There are a number of trustworthy options that you could consider before you decide on which outlet is ideal for purchasing the breed that you need. A hatchery might be the most obvious choice in this regard. It's easy to find one close to where you live, and since most have been in business for decades, the birds that are sold there come with quality guarantees. They also accept gender specific orders, which means that you could either buy roosters or hens, or a mix of both, based on your preferences. Many hatcheries in the US offer door-to-door delivery and pick-up services.

Farm supply stores and feed stores are also useful avenues for purchasing young chicks. While you may be able to make a decent bargain at these outlets, they do not often sell birds on specific gender orders. In other words, when you purchase from a farm supply or feed store, you can't be certain whether you will be delivered a box of roosters, hens, or both.

Animal swap meets at the community level can be a useful avenue to purchase chicken breeds that are in season. You must, however, make sure to check the health of the bird before you make your purchase, as such markets tend to deal in different animal species under one roof, and this can increase the possibility of contracting transmissible infections from other poultry or livestock. If you aspire to raise chickens as pets or for display in exhibitions, you might find the fancy supply that you need with a specialty breeder. Such individual chicken dealers maintain a stock of rare but spectacular bird varieties that might suit your needs perfectly. Animal shelters may also have a collection of chicken breeds that you could choose from. This alternative might be perfect for you if you believe in physically examining the birds before you buy them. Neighbors or friends who maintain a flock in their backyards or farms may also sometimes have the variety that you're looking for. Adopting a couple hens or roosters from such acquaintances may be just what you need to get your flock thriving. The web offers productive avenues to make smart purchases of rare as well as popular breeds. You could consider getting in touch with local chicken sellers through social media groups or even ordering your baby chicks from dedicated websites that tend to be most active around the onset of spring.

CHAPTER SUMMARY

- Brown layers, colored layers, and white layers are the primary heads of classification that are used to categorize the different breeds of chicken.
- Spring is the most ideal season to purchase and hatch baby chicks.
- You could purchase your flock from a hatchery, a farm supply or feed store, specialty breeders, neighbors, or even online.

2

THE ROOSTING BUDGET

The first thing that will occur to you when you think about translating your ambition of living a self-sufficient life into reality is the cost of maintaining a poultry farm. While the idea of owning a flock of chickens and consuming their fresh produce in the tranquil countryside can seem inviting, it is wise to educate yourself on the financial aspect of the practice as there are real costs associated with the process. You will have to invest your funds in purchasing the birds, building their coop, arranging for their feed, maintaining their health, and other miscellaneous expenses. When you put some thought into the amount of money that you might need for setting up and maintaining the infrastructure that a flock of chickens requires for its sustenance, you will not only be able to plan your finances well, but you'll also be able to avoid unnecessary expenditures. The rest of this chapter is dedicated to understanding the monetary aspect of raising chickens in your backyard or farm and to providing you with useful tips to ensure that you make judicious use of your time and resources.

THE COOP

The investment that you will need to make to erect a coop that is right for your flock is the most important financial consideration to take into account while preparing your poultry budget. A coop is the shelter in which you will likely house your birds after sunset, or even during the day if it has sufficient room for the little chickens to roam about freely. How much you will need to set aside for a chicken coop depends on a host of individual factors. The first parameter in this regard is the number of birds that you intend to bring home. You could begin with a flock of anywhere between 4 and 12 birds of the breed of your choice. Even if you start with a few hens and roosters at first, it is advisable to erect a coop that is larger than the immediate needs of your birds. This is because, with highly fertile breeds, you can expect to welcome baby chicks into your flock rather quickly, and the new birds will need sufficient room to grow and develop. The size of the chicken breed will also determine the amount of space that your coop must have on the inside. The larger the coop, the greater the cost in most cases, but you can expect to have a shelter for your birds ready for anywhere between $400 and $2,000, subject to various factors.

Chicken coops are of three distinct types.

A-Frame: This is a compact shelter that is ideal for four to six small or medium sized birds. You will be able to have no more than a couple of nesting boxes and roosts on the inside. Such coops may or may not have an attached run for your birds to wander about freely. Due to its small size, however, you may not be able to reach the deep interiors of the structure, and this can make maintenance a challenge. Depending on the materials used to construct an A-frame coop, you may have to set aside about $200 for the purpose, subject to other considerations. This type is most suitable for small flocks and for constrained spaces and budgets.

Tractor: This coop is larger in size and can easily accommodate upwards of eight medium-sized birds. Your chickens will nevertheless require free land to roam about during the daytime, as although this type is more spacious, it is not as big as a walk-in or an all-purpose coop. The most significant benefit of a tractor coop is its mobility. In other words, the wheels at the bottom of the shelter make it possible for you to change the location of your coop every now and then. The coop is large enough for it to be fitted with nesting boxes, roosts, and other season-specific requirements on the inside.

Walk-In: As the name suggests, these shelters are large enough to facilitate the free movement of not just the birds but also of the landowner. You will be able to access every corner of the coop, which will make maintenance and surveillance easy. This type of coop doesn't always come with an attached run, and therefore you will either need to build one or ensure that your birds have sufficient outdoor space to scour around in the fields during the daytime. You can expect to purchase a high-quality walk-in coop for anywhere between $650 and $1000, based on your preferred size, choice of material, structural design, and other associated costs.

Another coop variety that is in many ways a combination of the three types above is the all-in-one chicken shelter. It comprises the characteristics of an A-frame, a tractor, and a walk-in coop. Since its size is relatively large, you can experiment with more fancy designs for the shelter as opposed to a standard structure. An all-in-one coop will likely cost you upwards of $2000, subject to variation based on individual specifics.

Chicken coops can be erected with a host of different materials, and which one you choose will greatly determine the amount of money you end up spending on construction. You will need to select the material that is most suitable to cover the walls, the floor, the roof, and the frame of the shelter based on your individual circumstances. Softwood, redwood, and plywood are great options to consider in this aspect. They can be used on the walls and ceiling of the coop, as well as on its floor. While wood is an economical option, it is not the most maintenance-friendly material. It can be challenging to tidy up, and unless fitted appropriately, it can become a gateway for bugs and other infestations. A combination of mesh and plastic, PVC, is a great option for building a chicken coop as it's easy to lay, maintain, and afford. Lumber that is treated to be resistant to predators can also be used as the covering material for the roof and walls of the coop. If you are working on a tight budget, you can consider tin for your chicken shelter. If you live in a cool region, however, you may want to stay away from using tin in your coop, as it may not be able to keep your birds warm during the winters. Plastic, although a common component in ready-to-assemble chicken coops, is a rather expensive roofing material. It is comfortable for the birds to wander around on, and therefore you could incorporate it into your coop if you have generous financial resources for your poultry farm. Wooden frames work well as the flooring for a coop, particularly if you are building the structure without professional assistance. You must, however, remember to seal the flooring from all corners to prevent unwanted pests from entering the coop and infecting your birds. Rubber-based materials or sheets are ideal for a chicken shelter not only because they are extremely affordable but also because they suit the needs of the little birds perfectly. Vinyl is another inexpensive option to take into account when it comes to the coop's flooring. You could also choose wiring for this purpose, but you must be cautious enough to cover it with sand, sawdust, or other components that the birds will find easy to walk on. Chicken coops made of concrete are not uncommon on farms and in backyards. It might be more expensive than some of the other cost-effective coop materials, but it provides complete protection against predators. Mesh is, in most cases, an indispensable part of a chicken coop, as it is vital to cover the windows and sometimes even the surface of the shelter with it.

Another important cost parameter for a chicken coop, apart from its type and the material used, is the expense incurred in its construction. Unless you build the structure yourself, you will need to account for labor overheads while computing the total cost of your coop. If you choose to avail yourself of the services of a professional, perhaps a carpenter, you must add approximately $60–$80 per hour to the aggregate. Constructing a medium- to large-sized coop can take anywhere from four hours to a full work day. You can save upwards of $500 in labor costs if you opt to either order a coop kit, which will only require you to assemble the structure on the farm, or build the entire shelter yourself from scratch. Time and effort will be the only investments that you will have to make if you select the DIY route for erecting your coop. Choosing to convert an existing structure on the land, such as a shed, into a chicken shelter can help further reduce material costs as well as the time that it will take to get a coop ready. To sum up, while it is true that the possibilities with respect to a coop's design and size are endless, it is entirely feasible to build or buy a functional chicken shelter for anywhere between $500 and $800.

FENCING

The next important cost consideration in your poultry project is the money that you'll have to spend on fencing. You could choose to surround your flock with a fence, either as a primary layer of protection or as a secondary safety guard in addition to your coop. The proportion of your budget that you will have to dedicate to fencing will depend on the area that you need to cover as well as the material that you choose. Some of the different fencing options that you can consider as a landowner are as follows.

Wire fence: As is apparent from the title, this type of fencing involves surrounding your chicks with a boundary of wires. You could use one or more varieties of chicken wire to create the fencing barrier, as this will ensure greater control over predators and will also keep your birds within a designated area of your land. This is a highly economical way to protect your birds from unwanted intrusions. This type of fencing is especially ideal if your farm is exposed to dogs or other similar-sized mammals. A wired fence can also be created to serve as a tall barrier if you bring home a variety of chickens that tend to fly high or if you suspect that your flock might be at risk from aerial predators. Although this safety measure is easy to implement, as it is cheap and simple to install, the protection it offers to your birds is not full-proof. Snakes and other slimy insects may find their way in, and hence you will always have to be vigilant with this type of fencing.

Wire and wood fence: If you want your birds to be surrounded by a barrier that is more sturdy, you could opt for a wire and wood fence. The enclosure comprises closely assembled wires attached to a wooden frame. You may not be able to install a wood and wire fence without professional assistance, as the process necessitates extensive ground preparation in the form of digging and leveling. This fence variant can be modified to be taller to keep away aerial invaders, or it could be designed to be mobile, making it possible for you to disassemble the structure and move it elsewhere on the land when needed.

Chain-linked fence: In terms of the potential to keep predators away, this type of fencing is superior to the wired one, as it uses a network of closely interconnected chains that create a useful boundary for your birds. Instead of the usual hexagon-shaped openings that you see on farms and in backyard fences, this variety comprises smaller squares or circles. This will not only be a deterrent for smaller predators, but it will also turn out to be harder to break open for wild animals that may find their way to your chickens.

Net fence: Extremely inexpensive and easy to install, a net fence is ideal for a flock of chickens on a farm as well as in a garden or backyard. Since net as a material is relatively lightweight, there are both advantages and disadvantages to using it as a component of fencing. Its fragile texture makes it easy to handle for landowners, and its economical pricing means that it is unlikely to be out of your poultry budget, no matter how modest it may be. On the flip side, a net fence may not serve as a foolproof guard against predators, as most insects and bugs will find a way to penetrate through it eventually. Moreover, it is not the most ideal type of fencing for regions that experience harsh climatic conditions, as it has the tendency to disintegrate or fall apart during rain or snow storms. It is therefore important to evaluate the risks and benefits of using a net fence for your chickens before you introduce it to your land.

Pallet fence: Made with recycled wood, this type of fencing is a useful alternative to consider for your birds. It is easy to erect and maintain. It can be the perfect fencing option for you if you are working on a tight budget for your poultry project. It is important to note, however, that since pallet wood is difficult to dismantle, you must put in enough thought before you choose to install this fence on your farm as you may not be able to get rid of it with ease.

Electric fence: This protective boundary is commonly used on farmlands in the countryside, but you must incorporate it into your landscape only if you are unable to deal with predators and if they are causing destruction beyond normal agricultural losses. Although this option will eliminate invaders from entering your bird space altogether, you must attempt other alternatives to keep your chickens safe, as discouraging other animals from entering your land by putting them in danger of death due to electrification is unethical on many counts. Moreover, having to deal with electricity on a regular basis might be perilous for you as a landowner. Nevertheless, if you reside in a region where your baby chicks cannot thrive without an electric fence, you may consider surrounding your land with one. You will, however, need to set aside a significant sum as it is more expensive than some of the other fencing alternatives.

Plastic fence: This is a kind of fencing that can be used to house your birds on a temporary basis. Despite its affordability, a plastic fence isn't the most ideal enclosure, as predators can make their way into it remarkably easily. It can, however, prove to be a productive choice if your garden or backyard is naturally free of unwanted insects or bugs.

Enclosed fence: A wired, wooded, or net boundary that surrounds your birds on all four sides is known as an enclosed fence. This is most useful in regions that are at risk of attack by aerial invaders. Although you may not be able to build this enclosure yourself, its cost-effectiveness in the long-run will more than compensate for the labor expenses that you incur at the time of installation.

Subject to variation based on the area that you need to cover and the material that you choose, you can comfortably fence your birds for anywhere between $70 and $90. Another financial aspect that you have to consider with fencing is maintenance and repair. Quite often, fences lose their shape or they sag away because of attacks from predators, picking by your own birds, or unforeseen events like difficult weather conditions. Such loose ends will have to be fixed immediately, as not doing so can compromise the safety of your chickens. Hence, setting aside a few hundred dollars for fencing repairs each year is, in many ways, mandatory.

FEEDING

The cost of feeding your chickens is an important consideration when computing the total poultry budget that you need to set aside. While it's possible to reduce some of the other expenses that are associated with maintaining a flock of chickens, I encourage you to refrain from compromising on what you feed your birds for lack of finances. You could perhaps avoid the coop altogether and house your chickens in a fenced area of your land if you want to minimize the money you spend, but you must never feed them poor-quality food. What you feed your chickens will impact their health, and this will in turn impact the type of produce in terms of eggs and meat that you're able to generate from them. In general, the birds have a versatile and healthy diet. The funds that you need to allocate for this purpose will depend on how much feed your birds need. Certain breeds have greater nutritional requirements than others. The stage of life in which your birds find themselves will also impact the amount of feed that they'll need. For example, during the laying season, you may have to invest in high-protein feeds for your hens. You can reduce the feeding expenses of your birds by encouraging a diet of fruit and vegetable scraps, kitchen waste, and other such in-house alternatives. Taking these factors into consideration, you should expect to incur a monthly expenditure of close to $30 for a flock of five to six medium-sized chickens on average. Besides their regular diet of about a cup of soy beans, grains, or greens per day, your chickens will likely need to be nourished with additional supplements based on their individual requirements and health conditions. For example, if you live in a region that is deprived of natural sunlight for much of the year, your birds might become deficient in vitamin D, and therefore, you might need to compensate through artificial means. Moreover, just like we need to satiate our taste buds and occasionally eat something that satisfies our cravings, your chicks too need to be treated to special delicacies once in a while. These additions, apart from the regular feed, will cost you money, and in this context, it is wise to set aside about $150–$200 annually as miscellaneous expenses for dietary supplements and treats. This amount can be adjusted based on the number of birds you have, their breed type, size, health condition, stage of life, and so on. One way to economize on your feeding costs is to let your birds wander about freely on your farm or in your backyard. Exposing them to nature will mean that many of your chicks will find their own food in the form of flies, mosquitoes, or other insects. This will minimize the amount of protein that you will have to feed them in order to generate nutritious produce.

THE CHICKS

Needless to say, one of your first expenditures will be in purchasing the little birds. How much you'll need to spend in this aspect will depend on the breed you choose and where you reside, although chicken prices are quite consistent across most places in the United States. A baby chick can cost you anywhere between $1 and $5. Therefore, an initial flock of four birds will necessitate an investment of no more than $25. Adult birds tend to sell for prices between $15 and $30. The variation in the cost of a chicken is primarily dependent on the breed and how common or rare it is. Some endangered species of the bird, for instance, sell in the market for as much as $5,000. Also, hens always cost more than roosters. In short, a flock of four adult birds can be easily purchased for anywhere between $100 and $120. While this is a one-time expenditure, you will need to account for a recurring cost by way of having to replace your birds. Chickens have a lifespan of up to eight years, or even longer if well taken care of. However, their egg laying years only tend to last 2-3 years, so after this period is when they are often sent for slaughter. When they do die eventually, you'll have to purchase new birds to add to your flock if you choose not to hatch any of the eggs that your hens lay. Loss of baby chicks due to an attack by predators is another instance that will necessitate further financial investment in replenishing your flock. It is therefore wise to set aside approximately $100 for replacing your chickens each year. Bear in mind, though, that you will not have to spend that sum mandatorily on an annual basis as it's an event that will occur infrequently. Another alternative that you could consider is to buy eggs from the market and hatch them into baby chicks on your farm or in your backyard. While this route might appear more cost-effective because eggs are cheaper to purchase than chickens, beware that you must invest in an incubator for the hatching process. This will, in all certainty, be more expensive than buying a flock of hens and roosters from a hatchery or specialty dealer. Moreover, you will be unable to tell whether your eggs will hatch into roosters or hens, and this can disrupt your poultry plans drastically. Nevertheless, if you find it thrilling to see eggs turn into little chicks, or if you intend to hatch the fertile eggs produced from your backyard hens in the future, then you could give this alternative a try.

MISCELLANEOUS COSTS

Apart from the above expenses, you'll need to spend money on poultry accessories like nesting boxes, feeders, heating lamps, bedding, and waterers. Nesting boxes, which sell for approximately $30 each, are a must, for every hen needs her own private space to lay eggs. These can be placed inside the chicken coop along with the waterer, which you should be able to purchase for about five dollars. Nearly equal in cost is the feeder, which, when used, will ensure that your birds do not quarrel with one another for a share of the feed. It will also minimize food waste and reduce the time that you'll have to invest in cleanup every day. Heating lamps can generally be purchased from wherever you source your baby chicks; and when these accessories are bought in a package, they cost anywhere between $40 and $50. For an economical setup, you could convert the leftover pieces from the material that was used to construct the bird coop as bedding for the chickens. Another ongoing expense that you will have to incur throughout the life of your birds are the fees that you pay to your vet for consultation or treatment. This must be taken into account when you compute the total sum that you need to keep aside for miscellaneous expenses.

PURCHASING EGGS VS RAISING CHICKENS

When you consider the financial aspect of purchasing your poultry needs from the market or housing a flock of birds on your own farm or backyard, the first question that comes to mind is which of those alternatives is likely to be more economical. To understand this, let's assume that you are a family of four and you decide to adopt a flock of four mature birds. Aggregating the cost associated with the various heads that were discussed above, it will become clear that in order to purchase and maintain chickens for self-sustenance, you will need an initial investment of roughly $1300–$1500. Although this amount may seem significant on the face of it, it is important to put this total into context. The figure comprises a number of capital expenses, or costs that need to be incurred just once in your self-sustenance journey. For instance, from the second year on, you won't need to spend money on constructing the coop, building the fence, or purchasing the chicks. This will cut the cost of running your poultry farm in half. Moreover, if you choose cost-effective alternatives like erecting the coop yourself, feeding your birds kitchen scrap in addition to purchasing packaged food, you will be able to reduce your initial monetary outlay further. Many of the expenses that make up your financial budget for year two are variable in nature. For example, perhaps you feed your birds well and look after their health; this will mean fewer visits to the veterinarian. Likewise, if you manage to keep predators away, you will be able to eliminate many of the expenses that are connected with maintenance and repair. It is therefore clear that if you adopt a mindful approach toward maintaining your flock from the start, then pursuing a self-sufficient lifestyle is not that expensive after all. Assuming that you have a requirement of 12 eggs for a week as a family, you will invariably spend more than $200 each year in a grocery store. This is exclusive of the amount that you will shell out on travel, consumer taxes, purchasing meat from your local butcher, and so on. Moreover, practicing a self-sufficient lifestyle has benefits that extend beyond financial savings. The nutritional content and taste of farm-raised chicken produce are not comparable to the eggs and meat that are sold commercially. You will also be able to consume your favorite delicacies without feeling guilty for indirectly encouraging animal cruelty in slaughterhouses or negatively impacting the environment by purchasing poultry from markets that thrive on an extensive transportation network. The sense of fulfillment that you will derive from managing your own flock of birds and living off your own land is unmatched by any urban purchase or consumption experience. Therefore, consuming the fresh produce of your own flock will not only help you in elevating your lifestyle but also in uplifting the quality of your existence.

CHAPTER SUMMARY

- It's crucial to be aware of the costs associated with maintaining a poultry farm before you purchase a flock of hens and roosters.
- You will require adequate finances to buy chicks, build the infrastructure that they need for their survival on your land, and purchase the accessories that will help you maintain your flock in a healthy condition.
- Self-sufficiency has the potential to help you achieve financial, mental, and all-around satisfaction.

3

THE FOWL PLAY

Possessing knowledge on the various aspects of poultry farming before you push the gas pedal on raising chickens is paramount to ensure that you transition smoothly from your current way of existence to self-sufficiency. Staying prepared will not only help you in confronting the challenges that your new life presents, but it will also drive you toward achieving your desired objectives with respect to self-sustenance. An important facet of raising chickens on your farm or in your backyard, apart from educating yourself on the financial framework necessary for the purpose, is having a thorough understanding of the legal environment with respect to the practice in the region in which you reside. The rules regarding poultry farming will influence every dimension of your endeavor, from the type of birds that you might be permitted to bring home to the design of your coop or farm. The succeeding pages of this chapter delve deep into the laws that apply to raising chickens on farms, in gardens, or in backyards across the United States.

PERMITS AND LICENSES

Poultry farming in America is highly regulated, and systematic procedures are in place to ensure that the process of slaughtering the birds and using them as a food source is carried out in the right way. It's important to note that if you're raising poultry exclusively for personal consumption, you do not need to obtain any licenses from the regulatory authorities in America. On the contrary, if you aspire to use your chickens as a means to make profits from their sale, you will likely require a legal authorization of one kind or another. To become aware of which license is appropriate for you, you must define your poultry business in terms of the number of birds that you intend to slaughter, as well as how and to whom you aspire to sell their produce. The legal permits that are granted by authorities that regulate the business of poultry in America are as follows.

Special Permit

This license is granted by the Food Safety Program, and it might be right for you if you have short-term plans to sell your poultry produce. The license is issued to those landowners who intend to secure a legal poultry sanction for either one or two years. Another condition for receiving the authorization through this license is the number of birds that you slaughter in one calendar year. You will not be granted the special permit if you kill and sell over 1,000 birds in a year. Along with the application for the license, you will be required to pay a fee of $75 for one year, or $125 for a two-year authorization. The request for a special permit can be made either through email or by post. You may have to provide personal data like your name and address in addition to specific information about the slaughter process that you plan to implement and the storage facilities that you have or aspire to build on your land. The application will, in all probability, demand an architectural depiction of the storage and hygiene infrastructure that you have in place before you are granted the license to sell your produce. Scientific tests to establish the portability of water in terms of its quality are also mandatory in many states across the U.S.. The authorization purview of this license is limited to the sale of poultry to consumers, and you will not be allowed to process or swap chickens with it.

Federal License

This permit is necessary for those landowners who intend to raise and sell chickens at a commercial level. The procedure for obtaining the license is similar to the special permit, and you should be able to get an authorization for a period greater than two years through a single application. The United States Department of Agriculture is the granting authority for this permit.

Pet Bird or Poultry Importation Permit

As can be implied from the title, this license is necessary if you are importing chicks or eggs from a foreign country. You must obtain an import number from the agricultural department of the state in which you reside by providing relevant information pertaining to yourself as well as information about the breed that you want to bring home. The application can be delivered to the concerned authority by post or email. After the birds or eggs enter American shores, they will be held in quarantine for a specified period before they are released to their rightful owners once the department is satisfied with their health and safety.

Poultry Mortality Disposal Registration

This legal provision is concerned with the appropriate handling and disposal of chicken carcasses and eggs that cannot be consumed or sold. When your birds die or are slaughtered such that they are rendered unfit for commercial sale, it is your responsibility as the landowner to register their mortality with the relevant state-level agricultural authority in the region where you reside. In most cases, an application made to this effect with the appropriate legal body serves as sufficient compliance of the provision. The United States Department of Agriculture has laid down several regulations that must be abided by when disposing of dead poultry from your farm or backyard. The carcasses must be suitably dealt with within 48 hours of the bird's death, and you could choose from the many disposal methods that are provided by the USDA. Since chickens are relatively small in size, the U.S. Department of Agriculture allows for their carcasses to be turned into compost or into other useful farm fertilizers. You could also opt to lay your diseased birds to rest in an authorized burial site, or you could reduce them to ashes in a controlled and enclosed environment. Rules in this regard vary between states in America, and hence, it's wise to check for specific legal provisions with the extension office of the agricultural department of your region beforehand.

Intensive Poultry Operation Permit

If you intend to carry out intensive poultry operations as defined in the agricultural regulations of the United

States on your farm, you will require a permit before you begin the practice. You will need to make an application to the commissioner of the agricultural department of your state. Not every regional office provides for online submissions, and therefore, it is best to check with the concerned authority beforehand. In addition to the fee for obtaining the license, you may be required to provide a surety of a few thousand dollars to the commissioner of the agricultural department. As a landowner, it is important to be prepared for an inspection by the commissioner, who will attempt to evaluate your facilities in light of the necessary requirements of intensive poultry operations in America. If your premises meet the mandatory standards prescribed by the act, you will be granted a license for the desired activity. It is vital to retain the standards of infrastructure that got you the authorization for as long as you carry out intensive poultry operations on your land, as the commissioner has the right to cancel the sanction if deficiencies are observed during subsequent inspections.

Poultry Live Dealer License

As the owner of a poultry farm, you are obligated to seek this permit if you plan to sell live chickens or hatching eggs. This license is necessary even if you only intend to handle living birds either as a wholesaler or any other intermediary before the chicks reach the end user. The permit is granted on an annual basis and can be obtained from your regional agricultural office. The regulation that deals with the trade in this type of poultry in America mandates certain standards with respect to the handling of the birds, their transport, and their sale in live markets. You risk losing your permit if you fail to abide by the provisions of the law with respect to these parameters. The procedure to make a request for the license is fairly simple. You will need to provide the required information via an online application form to the regional office of the agricultural department where you intend to deal in or sell live poultry.

Registering Your Flock

Although not mandatory in most states across America, getting your flock registered with the regional agricultural office is a wise choice for a number of reasons. Firstly, you will receive a premises identification number upon registration, and this will come in handy every time you claim benefits that you might be entitled to from the concerned authority, as well as when you display your birds in exhibitions or rural fairs. When you manage a registered flock of hens and roosters, you will be informed of potential health risks to your chicks from circulating viruses or other ailments in the poultry community. You can also seek and receive guidance on managing your breed better and making the most of prospective opportunities to gain more from your flock by participating in rural contests or exhibits.

Selling Live Birds, Hatching Eggs, or Table Eggs

The only lawful way to make money from the sale of live chickens, hatching eggs, or shell eggs is to obtain a license from the agricultural department that has authority in the region in which you live. A sanction is necessary even if you sell these items directly to the end user. Authorizations are likewise mandatory, not only for selling table eggs, but also when importing them from a foreign country. You must remember to abide by the regulations pertaining to the storage and transport of live chickens and eggs in order to avoid facing the untoward consequences of legal violations.

Poultry Swap Meat Policy

Licensing requirements for participating in regional poultry swap meet events are unambiguously prescribed in the agricultural legislation in America. These formally arranged meets offer poultry owners the opportunity to exchange their chicks for a monetary value. You will, however, need to possess a permit to deal in live birds, as well as the authorization that recognizes your poultry premises, in order to participate and benefit from these events.

National Poultry Improvement Plan (NPIP)

An initiative of the United States Department of Agriculture, the program was introduced with the intention of improving the health of poultry and reducing the transmission of communicable diseases among domesticated flocks. As an individual landowner, you are entitled to participate in the plan, which establishes chicken health standards by administering tests for common diseases caused by microorganisms. When it was first created in 1935, the NPIP intended to eliminate salmonella and other related disease-causing pathogens from among hens and roosters. Today, the plan covers a host of ailments, including but not limited to influenza, bacterial infections causing white diarrhea, respiratory illnesses, and so on. Many states in America mandate that only the birds that have received accreditation from NPIP with respect to their health can be transported within their borders. The provisions of the plan apply equally to the imports of chickens from foreign countries. The NPIP initiative is beneficial not only for the birds themselves but also for the intermediaries involved in raising poultry, from the landowner to the hatchery, as it ensures the handling, storage, transportation, and consumption of healthy meat and eggs. To obtain a medical certification for your flock from the NPIP, you will need to approach an authorized poultry testing agent from your regional agricultural department office. These trained individuals will collect blood samples from your birds and forward them to the NPIP laboratory for testing and analysis. Once your flock is found to be free of disease-causing microbes, you will receive the NPIP certification to this effect.

Consequences of Operating Without the Necessary Permits and Licenses

If you carry out any activity on your poultry farm that needs to be authorized by a federal license or permit without obtaining one, you risk facing unwanted consequences. Laws are in place to regulate the poultry industry to maintain the quality of the produce that the end users have access to, and also to ensure the well-being of all those who might even be only indirectly involved in the practice. When you raise chickens in your backyard, garden, or farm, your neighbors in the vicinity will, in all certainty, be affected by it. When you function with the necessary permits, you will save yourself from the ill consequences of causing discomfort to the public in general or to the vulnerable sections of the population. What's more, the United States Department of Agriculture can initiate legal action against your poultry practices if it discovers that you are functioning beyond the permitted scope of operation in the region where you reside. This can take the form of monetary fines or a forced closure of your poultry business. It is, therefore, in the best interest of your venture and self-sufficiency ambitions that you seek and obtain the necessary legal sanctions before you engage in any practice in the poultry industry.

LOCAL ORDINANCES

Traditionally, when the practice of raising chickens was restricted to the countryside, federal laws were sufficient to regulate the business. As awareness of the benefits of poultry farming grew, and as people began to embrace the self-sufficient way of life, hens and roosters started to appear in urban setups. There are a number of reasons why the presence of chickens in cityscapes can be disturbing, and therefore, new local ordinances were introduced by the different American states to regulate the raising of these birds in gardens or backyards. The risk of disease transmission from animals to humans was a matter of prime concern while poultry rules were being formulated by urban administrations. While it is true that potentially severe illnesses can spread from animals to humans when they are in close contact with one another, the danger from chickens is relatively marginal in this aspect. This is because of the generally small flocks that are maintained in urban households. Moreover, in spaces that house chicks, pests like cockroaches, ticks, mice, and other rodents tend to grow in population. Since this can have undesirable consequences not only for the birds themselves but also for the neighborhood, several states introduced restrictions on the flock size and their mode of maintenance. Loud noises and foul odors from chickens were two other important factors in the differences in legal ordinances between the various American states. The sounds created by roosters as they crow away all through the day and by hens when they lay eggs can be disturbing in urban residential areas. When chicken waste is not managed in an optimal manner, it can create unpleasant smells that can spread throughout the vicinity. Hence, a number of American counties introduced specific provisions for the treatment of chicken poop and its alternate use as compost or agricultural manure. On all these accounts, the county administrations in America enacted restrictive laws relating to poultry farming in urban settings. Many urban setups in the US either do not permit roosters in backyards or gardens of residential areas, or they require the owners to seek special permits for the same. Restrictions on the size of the coops that can be built for the birds are also common across the nation.

As a landowner, it is important for you to be aware of the specific poultry ordinances that apply in the territory in which you reside. The rules that are applicable to the raising of chickens in urban households in some of the prominent American states are discussed below.

New York

The state does not have any limitations with respect to the number of hens that you can house in your garden or backyard. County regulations for raising poultry in New York simply mandate that you abide by the standards of care and maintenance for the birds as prescribed by the United States Department of Agriculture. You will, however, need to be cautious about potential complaints from your neighbors, as these are taken extremely seriously by the administration of the state. Sharing the fresh produce of your birds with those in your vicinity might be a useful trick to avoid facing such issues.

Texas

Laws relating to raising chickens in backyards are numerous and rather complex in Texas. There are plenty of limitations imposed on the practice, and it is best to contact the regional agricultural office before attempting any poultry related activity in the state.

New Jersey

The authority that regulates the raising of poultry in households in New Jersey imposes regulations on the size and structure of the coop, as well as on how much noise from backyard flocks will be deemed acceptable by those in charge. A number of ordinances with respect to poultry are issued in the state on a regular basis, and more and more of these are in favor of encouraging residents to raise their own flock of chicks and to work toward self-sufficiency.

Oregon

Prospective chicken owners in the state must obtain a special permit for maintaining a flock that comprises in excess of three birds in their garden or backyard. You must also ensure that you have sufficient space on your farm for not only the coop itself but also to adequately distance the chicken shelter from other residential properties, as the state stipulates specific rules in this aspect.

Michigan

While much of the state is fairly liberal regarding raising chickens, the city of Detroit is a marked exception, as housing the birds in your backyard is entirely forbidden there. This regrettable state of affairs in the city might alter for the better in the near future, for poultry enthusiasts continue to push hard for a change in legislation in this regard.

Illinois

Residents of this state can bring home both hens and roosters without any restrictions on the type of breed, the number of birds, or the size of the coop. Despite this, it is ideal to adopt roosters with caution, as complaints from neighbors are taken very seriously. Illinois might not be best suited for raising chickens if your objective behind bringing home the birds is to consume their meat. This is because slaughtering is not permitted in residential areas in the state. Hens can, however, be held as pets as well as used for their eggs without any restrictive laws.

Since different counties have varied rules on raising, selling, and using poultry for their produce or as pets, it's important to get in touch with your city office or Town Hall beforehand. The informed individuals at these agricultural centers will be able to assist you with what is and is not permitted in terms of chickens in your locality. The aspect of managing poultry in an urban setting that most residents are usually unhappy with is either the odor of the chicken waste or the noise of the birds. You could mitigate the same by learning to handle chicken waste appropriately, avoiding roosters from your flock, and communicating openly with your neighbors about your objective behind raising chickens and how they could benefit from the practice. Involving the members of your neighborhood and sharing the fruits of your labor with them can make it easy to own a flock of birds in a bustling urban setup.

Consequences of Violation of Local Ordinances

Like every other civil infringement, not following the rules that are applicable to the practice of raising poultry in a city will have negative repercussions. The immediate consequence of the violations of legal poultry provisions will likely be complaints from those in your locality. This can later precipitate monetary fines and other non-monetary penalties. In order to ensure the uninterrupted continuity of the practice of raising your own chickens and progressing toward a self-sufficient way of life, it is important to operate in accordance with the rules that are in force wherever you live.

Health and Safety Regulations

These laws apply to poultry owners who aspire to sell their homegrown produce. Before you make profits from your self-raised flock, you will need to obtain an authorization from the health department of your state. This permit guarantees the safety of your meat or eggs in terms of their potential impact on human health.

The license is granted if the produce is found to be of high quality and fit for consumption. These regulations are vital as they ensure that unnecessary health complications do not result from consuming domestically produced meat or eggs. The possibility of the outbreak of diseases within communities or even cities from infected poultry are minimized greatly when you obtain a health permit from the local authority before engaging in the sale of your farm produce.

Disease Prevention Regulations

Maintaining a healthy flock of birds is paramount to sustaining your poultry business in the long-run. You'll be unable to achieve your self-sufficiency ambitions if your hens and roosters are diseased or immunocompromised. Therefore, regulations are established in the form of biosecurity, vaccinations, and infrastructure specifications for the well-being of your flock. In simple terms, biosecurity encompasses everything you do to keep your chickens healthy. It refers to every attempt you make as a landowner to eliminate the presence of microbes or other pathogens from your farm. Fencing your land to safeguard your birds from terrestrial predators or testing your water source to ensure that it meets the standards prescribed by the Department of Agriculture in America are both examples of biosecurity measures. Additional steps that you could take to keep your birds in good health include establishing procedures for routine cleaning of the coop, disposing of the carcasses of dead chicks within 48 hours, prohibiting transportation vehicles from entering your farm space, storing feed in a hygienic manner, ensuring that all persons dealing with the birds do so with tidy hands and sanitized clothing, creating rules for handling the produce of your poultry business in the correct way, maintaining the shelter and all other required infrastructure in good condition, and so on. Such biosecurity measures will serve as the primary protection medium for your birds, and they will make the secondary safety mechanism of administering disease-preventing vaccines to your chicks all the more effective. As a landowner, it will only benefit your poultry practice if you abide by the regulations of biosecurity, shed infrastructure, and bird vaccination as issued by the state in which you reside.

Regulations for the Use of Medications and Supplements

While you may have an ambition to raise organic produce from your backyard flock, it's important to understand the laws relating to the use of prohibited substances on chicks. This is because there will be instances in your journey as a poultry owner in which your birds might not be in the best of health. These occasions will necessitate the use of antibiotics and other medications based on the illness that your bird or flock is suffering from. Even if you're a certified producer of organic meat and eggs, legal provisions do not prevent you from administering such drugs to your sick birds when they genuinely need them. The only agricultural requirement in this aspect is that the birds that have been treated with non-organic means cannot be sold or marketed as organic products. The medical regulations for poultry allow the use of approved medicines, either individually or in permitted combinations, in the event of infection in the flock. There are also a number of scientifically backed medicated feeds that you could use in addition to the routine ration that you provide as food to your chicks on a daily basis. It is vital to remember in this context that such feeds must be procured from licensed vendors and that the instructions on the packaging must be followed with precision.

Animal Welfare Regulations

These laws relating to poultry have been established to ensure that the birds are treated well by their owners. This pertains to the primary requirements of the chicks, namely food, shelter, and medication. The legal provisions for animal welfare stipulate that every hen or rooster in your flock must have access to adequate and nutritious feed and high-quality drinking water at all times. Chickens are naturally mobile creatures, and they need to stay active in order to enjoy good health and produce fine eggs and meat. Therefore, the welfare laws focus on the size of the coop in terms of the amount of space that must be available for each bird based on its breed type, size, and personality. Your birds should be permitted to range freely all through the day, and they must not be confined to cramped spaces. It is deemed ethical practice as per the animal welfare regulations to treat diseased birds with special care. All efforts must be made, either through medications or otherwise, to restore the chickens to good health.

Slaughter Regulations

As a poultry owner, you must create the infrastructure that is necessary to slaughter chickens in your backyard or farm. There must be established processes for the slaughtering, handling, transportation, and sale of the birds. If you intend to kill chickens for direct sale to customers and if their number does not exceed 1,000 in one calendar year, you may be able to operate without a state or federal license in most parts of America. In all other cases, you will need to obtain the necessary permits and the applicable inspection exemptions to continue the practice uninterrupted.

CHAPTER SUMMARY

- It is important to become aware of the legal framework surrounding the practice of poultry management before you begin your chicken raising journey.
- There are a number of federal and state licenses that need to be obtained based on the nature of the activities that you undertake on your farm.
- Failing to comply with applicable regulations can have undesirable consequences, which can sometimes lead to the closure of your poultry business.

4

A HAPPY HEN HOUSE

Since chickens are highly adaptable creatures, you may be tempted to let them free range without providing them with a shelter of their own. This is especially true when you are working on a budget or if you are new to poultry farming. However, the time and finances that you invest in erecting a chicken coop in your backyard have multiple benefits. It's even necessary for the birds on many counts as chickens are fragile birds and they need protection. A coop will help them stay safe as it will help to keep predators away and will also shield them from unpredictable nature. Poultry activities like roosting, laying eggs, and feeding can be accomplished inside the shelter. This will not only keep your farm organized, but it will also aid you in better flock management. To sum up, having a separate chicken shelter will ensure that you raise birds that are happy, healthy, productive, and stress-free.

COOP DESIGN PLANS

Whether you are building one yourself or purchasing a ready-made coop from a store, the possibilities with respect to the design, size, and structure of a chicken shelter are endless. A good coop must nevertheless comprise the following features.

Location: Make sure that the chicken shelter is situated fairly close to your house. This will make monitoring and egg collection easy. Erect or place the coop away from your garden so as to prevent the birds from spoiling your vegetation. The shelter must be so situated that it receives a fair share of sunlight and shade throughout the day.

Size: Adequate room is paramount for a chicken to thrive happily. Each bird requires a minimum of 2 square ft. of space within the coop. For larger breeds, the number may increase to up to 5 square ft. You must compute the size of the shelter that your flock will require depending on the breed type and the number of birds you bring home. About 10 square ft. of space for one bird is necessary on the attached run. Chickens are social creatures, and they need to be adequately entertained in order to be healthy. You could consider adding dust bathing areas within the coop, for example. Remember, however, to take into account the space that will be necessary to accommodate such poultry engagement activities while calculating your coop size. Chickens will need nesting boxes and roosts within their shelter, so accounting for them when selecting your coop design is also vital.

Flooring: Materials like concrete, wood, and dust work well as the floor of a chicken shelter. Each of them has its own set of advantages and disadvantages in terms of cost, durability, and installation process. It is important that you choose the material that suits your individual circumstances with respect to your budget, predator risk, flock size, climatic conditions, and breed type.

Predator protection: The most important purpose that your chicken shelter must serve is to keep your birds safe from predators. It's crucial to understand the threats that your flock faces in your area. For example, if you fear attacks from wild birds, you should consider employing a covered run. Likewise, you could opt for an elevated coop if ground insects are your chicken's greatest enemies.

Foraging area: Wandering about in the wild and scratching around for prey is a chicken's inherited behavior. Providing space around the coop for foraging is a good idea to keep your flock happy and healthy. It is, however, vital to guard the birds from adverse climatic conditions. Creating a windbreak, in the form of a row of trees, for example, will protect the birds from excessive breeze and sunlight.

Fencing and doors: A chicken coop requires fencing and access outlets to be functional and easy to clean. The type of fencing you choose will depend on your individual circumstances in terms of the climate, the kind of predators that you are likely to encounter, and so on. Your shelter must also have a secure gate. The door, along with the windows, if applicable, must have locks that bolt correctly and cannot be easily broken by smart predators like foxes.

Ventilation: A good chicken shelter is one that allows for a free flow of air in and out of the structure. Windows can help immensely with ventilation, but if your local weather does not permit you to have them, you could consider installing vents or a fan on the inside. Keeping the air in the coop fresh is vital to maintaining the birds' good health.

Coop accessories: Chickens prefer to lay in dark and small spaces, so providing nesting boxes in your shelter is mandatory if you are raising the birds for their eggs. Remember to designate space for dust bathing and vertical room for perches for the birds to roost on at night. If the area where you live experiences harsh winters, you may require heating lamps to keep the birds warm as well as to make up for the absence of natural light during those days. A feeder for the birds can be placed inside the shelter or near the run to reduce food clutter. The chicken shelter must also contain bedding for the birds. The coop, along with the accessories, must create a spacious and secure environment for not only your birds to thrive in but also for you to be able to venture inside to collect eggs, clean, and manure every now and then.

DESIGN IDEAS

The following are some of the structural designs that you could consider for your chicken shelter.

Elevated coop: This structure has a greater amount of vertical room, or elevation, off the ground. It's ideal if you're worried of burrowing predators and insects. Another advantage is the prevention of high moisture inside the coop, especially if your area is susceptible to run-off or flooding.

Walk-in coop: The defining feature of this design is its large size, which enables poultry owners to easily enter, collect eggs, and clean the shelter.

Coop with planter: A marginally different chicken shelter design, this coop comprises additional aesthetic features like planters on the inside.

Room to run coop: This design eliminates the need to have a separate run, as the large size of the shelter means that the birds can engage in stress-relieving activities right there.

Rhode Island Red Eye Saloon: A compact and well-organized design structure, this is ideal for city homes.

Loft-style coop: The vertical structure of this design makes it ideal for a large flock that needs to be accommodated in a confined space.

Spacious retreat: This shelter is large in size, and the design facilitates the addition of all poultry accessories like roosts and a dust bath within the structure.

Chicken barn: This design is ideal for a large farm or backyard.

Chicken tractor: The portable nature of this structure makes this coop style extremely attractive as you can give your chickens fresh grass each time you move it and allow the grass to regrow in the area used previously. Its size is best suited for raising only a few chickens, however.

Modern roost: This coop design focuses on light and ventilation. It is ideal for regions that have a hot and humid climate.

Garden loft: With plenty of vertical room, this type of coop can easily fit into a garden of any size.

Efficient design: This chicken shelter aims to comfortably accommodate more birds in a small space.

Chicken shed: A cost-effective alternative, this design is ideal to put an existing farm space to good use.

As a new poultry owner, if you are daunted by the prospect of creating or choosing a coop design for your birds, you could consider using some of the freely available structural blueprints online. These detailed plans cover everything from the size to the material that you will need to construct the chicken shelter yourself.

An additional option you may consider is designing a coop based on the plans I've provided for you in this book. You'll find a blueprint of the coop design I used in my own backyard. It has served me and my chickens extremely well for the past decade. You can easily download the coop plans by scanning the QR code below. You'll find the same QR code at the end of this book as well.

WEATHERPROOFING YOUR CHICKEN COOP

Ensuring that your poultry shelter is safe for habitation during every season is extremely vital for the good health of your birds. A cool space during the summers and a warm aboard during the winters will keep your birds happy and stress-free. A number of easy steps will help you create a shelter that is just right for every weather type.

Step one: Assemble or build the coop in the part of your farm that receives abundant sunlight and ensure that the front of your shelter faces the east. This will help you maintain the henhouse in a dry condition. Remember to use a slanting roof for your coop if you reside in a region that receives plenty of rain or snow. This will create a natural drain path for the melting snow or water, thus keeping your shelter dry. Consider elevating your coop if your land is at risk of regular flooding.

Step two: Fix any cracks, holes, gaps, openings, or other compromised edges of the shelter with water-proofing material. You could use liquid rubber seam tape, a pond shield, or a waterproof sealant for this purpose.

Step three: Add heaters or heat lamps to the shelter as necessary, depending on the severity of the winter that your region experiences. Covering the walls of the coop with a thick cloth or a commercially available insulator is a good idea to keep your shelter warm and dry.

Step four: If the floor of your coop tends to get very cold or moist during the winters, you could temporarily cover it with more chicken bedding. This will keep your birds warm and your coop dry.

Step five: If your shelter design does not include windows, you may want to add vents or fans to facilitate better air circulation and keep your chickens healthy.

THE STRUCTURE

If you opt to order a ready-to-assemble coop, then all you will need to do is put the structure together by following the instructions on the product. On the contrary, if you decide to build one yourself, the process will require a greater investment in terms of your time and effort. Choosing the right material for your chicken shelter is the first task that you will need to accomplish. Plywood, hardwood, softwood, plastic, PVC, pallets, or even recycled material can work well for the coop. Which one of these you select will depend on your budget, the weather, the size of your flock, and so on. You must begin by constructing the frame for the main structure as well as for the run. A carpenter's toolkit should be sufficient to construct the coop yourself. For the walls of the chicken shelter, you can choose either wood or pallets. Likewise, for the roof, metal or pallets work perfectly. You can cut out windows or vents in the structure once it is built. Attach the run to the main structure and fence it with either wood, chicken wire, chain links, a hardware cloth, an electric net, or any other material of your choice. Finally, add the nesting boxes, the dust bath, and the perches to the coop. Your self-made chicken aboard is now ready for habitation by the little feathery creatures.

Special note: To assist you with the process, there are a number of online tools that let you create the design of your coop as a 3-D model. SketchUp, DreamPlan, AutoCAD, and Blender are some useful avenues in this regard.

CHAPTER SUMMARY

- A chicken coop is necessary for the birds to thrive.
- A good chicken shelter is one that provides protection from predators, is perfect to live in in every season, and is spacious enough to accommodate the entire flock.
- When building a chicken shelter, first construct its frame, then erect the walls, and finally fix the roof.

5

BECOMING A MOTHER HEN

When you first bring home a flock of chickens, you might fret about how best to care for them. This is because you understand the importance of nurturing your birds and the positive impact it can have on their well-being. What you may be innocently unaware of, however, is the benefit that owning and raising backyard chickens can have on your own health. It's known to provide social and emotional benefits to the owner, and a sense of fulfillment during and after the process. The succeeding pages of this chapter are dedicated to bringing to light the necessary aspects of caring for the little creatures that you must know as a poultry keeper.

THE FEED

What your chickens consume will determine the kind of produce that you generate from them. An easy and cost-effective alternative in this aspect is to let your birds find their own food in your backyard or farm. While this natural approach to chicken feeding might work just fine, you won't be able to control the diet of your birds if you adopt this method. To ensure that your baby chicks grow up into the kind of birds that you want them to, you could select one of the many feed options available in the market.

Starter feed: Highly rich in protein, this grain mixture is ideal for chicks until they are four to six weeks old. It has the right nutritional content to stimulate growth in baby chicks, and its powdery texture makes it easy to consume for the nascent birds.

Grower feed: You could transition to this feed after your birds have matured into medium-sized hens or roosters. This mixture is available in different textures, and you could use its pellets to introduce a change in your birds' daily feed.

Layer feed: Use this mixture for your hens during the laying season. Since it's high in calcium, the feed is not necessary for roosters or hens that do not lay eggs.

Broiler feed: The mixture brings about a sudden and difficult-to-control growth spurt in birds, even when used in small quantities. You must consider administering this feed to your flock only if you plan to slaughter the chickens for meat in the short-term.

Corn feed: This inexpensive mixture is well suited to those working with a relatively small poultry budget. However, it should not be used for a long period of time as it does not comprise the different nutrients that your birds need for their healthy development. The feed can be used occasionally and in combination with other alternatives.

Raiser feed: A kind of all-purpose mixture, the feed works well for both hens and roosters. It can be used daily if you are raising your chickens simply as pets, but it may not be able to stimulate your birds to lay eggs or to grow large enough to be used for meat.

Game bird feed: This mixture aids in building visually pleasing external features in chickens. You can try this variety if you plan to display your birds in shows or exhibits.

While most of the mixtures can be administered as they are, you are free to explore other modifications as well. For example, you could soak your feed in warm water overnight and use the fermented grains to nourish your birds the following day. Aside from these packaged feeds, you could create a diet of kitchen scraps and natural proteins like insects and farm bugs for your birds. It is, however, important to be mindful of the foods that might be potentially harmful to chickens. Certain items, like citrus fruits, may appear perfectly edible from a generic viewpoint, but they lead to a decline in fertility in hens. Many other foods, such as the skin of uncooked green potatoes and apricots, apple seeds, and chocolate, cause adverse toxic reactions in chickens, and they can also be fatal in many instances. Other food items that you must keep your birds clear of include onions, wild mushrooms, horseradish, tulips, ivy leaves, tomato plants, and raw beans. Not every plant, particularly those that are rare or largely ornamental, is fit for consumption by chickens. It is therefore best to consult your veterinarian before including unusual food substances in your birds' diet.

Economizing Feed Costs

Packaged feed mixes that are available in the market are effective for stimulating healthy growth in your birds, but they can also prove to be expensive in the long-run. Relying exclusively on this mode of feeding can put a tremendous strain on your poultry budget. Fortunately, there are a number of steps that you can take to minimize costs and still supplement your chickens with the right nutrition. The most effective approach in this aspect is to feed your birds a combination of packaged poultry food and grains that are available at home. Adding some rice or millet to their everyday ration will cut down on the expenses incurred in purchasing ready-made feeds, and it will also boost their overall health. Another way to make feeding more cost-effective, you could consider growing these grains on your farm yourself. If you have the space and resources to do so, then cultivating cereals, vegetables, and fruits on your land can help you manage your finances better. Fermenting chicken feeds before they are administered to your birds will help reduce the expenses involved with food, as the healthy bacteria in the mixture will keep the chickens full for longer. As was stated earlier, including kitchen scraps or leftover food in your chickens' diet can aid in cost reduction. Encouraging your hens and roosters to wander about the fields will ignite their natural instincts to search for and find their own prey. A direct consequence of this practice will be a reduced need to purchase poultry feed often. Investing in a feeder will help prevent food waste caused by chickens scattering the grains while they battle with one another for a share of the feed. While it's important to supplement the diet of your birds with occasional treats, the practice can become a burden on your budget if it is not done in a calculated manner. Feeding your birds too much will have negative repercussions, both for their health and for your wallet. By adopting the useful strategies that were discussed above, you will be able to feed your chickens well and also save money, which can be put to more productive uses in your poultry business.

PREDATORS

A crucial element of raising chickens is having the necessary measures in place to ensure that your chickens remain safe. Their small size and relatively innocent personalities make them highly susceptible to attacks from predators. While there are a number of steps that you can take to ensure the safety of your flock and its produce, understanding the specific threats that your birds face will make the attempt all the more successful. For instance, some regions in America have a greater risk of rat or mice infestations when compared to the rest of the country. When you are aware of who the enemy is, you will be able to introduce safety measures that will be more effective in keeping your chickens safe. Outlined below are some of the strategies that you could consider.

The Coop

The part of a poultry farm's infrastructure that needs your greatest attention when it comes to the safety of your chicks is their shelter. It must be made of a material that provides a secure interior for your birds. The walls, ceiling, and floor of the shelter must be free of cracks, small holes, or other loose ends. You must remember to check the structure regularly to identify and remedy such unwanted openings in your chicken coop before predators take advantage of them. Ventilation outlets must be constructed along the highest vertical of the shelter. You could fence your coop to prevent large predators, like foxes, from climbing up to these openings and harming your chicks while they're fast asleep. Your chicken shelter must have an exit that can be bolted, as you will likely need to lock up your birds in the shelter at night to keep them safe. It is best to use a covered run in regions that are susceptible to attacks by aerial predators. Technology in the form of sensors and motion detection cameras can keep you informed about the whereabouts of your birds when you aren't supervising them. They can be programmed to sound an alarm every time animal footsteps are detected, and this should be enough to drive away most predators. To keep away snakes and other reptiles that can eat up eggs and sometimes even your chicks, it is vital to invest some thought into the location of your coop on your land. It must be rather secluded and situated away from wild vegetation or clusters of trees or bushes.

Lighting

Chicken predators are most active during the night, as darkness serves as an excellent shield against the risk of being spotted before they catch their prey. In this context, it would be wise to ensure that the area around your coop is sufficiently lit after sunset. You could consider installing a solar lighting system to serve this purpose more economically. Adequate lighting will help to keep most predators away.

Predator Traps

If you fear that your flock might be at risk from stubborn invaders like snakes that keep returning to your coop despite all your efforts, you may need to use animal traps. These are different for different predators, and you could procure them from your local market. You could also use household tricks like splashing a dash of vinegar around your chicken shelter to deter snakes and other reptiles from approaching it. Many animals are intimidated by certain sounds, and you could use these noise deterrents to keep your birds safe. If you use a trap that might be fatal to predators, however, it is important to check with the legal provisions in your area before you introduce it on your land, as it can be unlawful to kill certain endangered animal species.

Hygiene

Cleaning your coop and its surroundings is an excellent way to keep predators at bay. Unconsumed feed, chicken waste, and other litter can attract rats, which can create an unnecessary nuisance on your land once they find a way to penetrate through your biosecurity protection. You must therefore make it a practice to maintain proper hygiene and to clean up chicken poop and other scattered grains before they begin to lure in predators.

Guard Animals

Domesticated pets like dogs can protect your chickens from predators. It is, however, important to become certain about the intentions of your dog or cat before you trust it with keeping your birds safe at night. This is because dog attacks on chickens simply for the thrill of it are not uncommon. Once your pet has proven its trustworthiness, though, you can rely on these four-legged creatures to do all they can to drive away nocturnal predators. Having a rooster in your flock can also help with spotting predators before they wage deadly attacks on your hens. Roosters are vigilant, and they have a keen eye for invaders. They are protective of their flock, and they generally alert their hens by crowing aloud when they sense danger. Hence, if roosters are legally permitted in the area in which you reside, having one for every seven hens is a productive alternative to keeping invaders in check.

Note: Predators are most active during the spring season, and therefore, you may need to use intensive poultry protection strategies at that time. Also, changing your approach to ensure the safety of your birds is important, as many animals can find their way around routine defense measures. While it's important to be informed about the various kinds of threats that your chicks might face during their existence, it is vital to refrain from procrastinating about losing your birds or eggs to such invaders. Doing some research on the predator population in your area and communicating with other landowners in the vicinity on the subject can help you devise a suitable predator detection strategy for your flock. Chickens are known to consume their own eggs in exceptional circumstances, so you may not need to immediately fret about invaders every time a fresh hatch goes missing. Possessing knowledge and practicing vigilance are the most crucial aspects of keeping your birds safe.

DISEASES

Just like every other living organism, chickens are susceptible to various kinds of ailments. Understanding the causes and symptoms of many of these diseases can help you treat your sick birds in time and maintain a happy flock. The health complications in chickens can be grouped as follows.

Behavioral Diseases

When a chicken is suffering from any of these issues, their presence can be understood by examining the bird's behavior. If one or more of the hens or roosters in your flock appear unusually lazy, reluctant to eat, or in pain, you can associate these signs with a probable underlying cause. Cuts or injuries to their feet, or bruises created by pecking, are the most common reasons behind behavioral diseases. Dressing the wounds on their legs and reducing pecking by ensuring that the chicks do not quarrel for space or are not overly stressed are simple solutions to these problems.

Metabolic Diseases

These internal malfunctions generally translate externally as a reduced capacity to lay eggs in hens. A variety of factors, from simple deficiencies to more complicated reproductive disorders, can lead to metabolic problems. If you aren't able to manage the issue by boosting the calcium and protein content in the feed of the hens, then you may need to see a veterinarian, who should be able to correct the biological defect through more complex interventions.

Infectious Diseases

A host of microorganisms like bacteria, viruses, and fungi can cause problems in chickens. It's vital to spot the symptoms of these illnesses quickly and treat the ailment before it infects your entire flock. Some of the communicable poultry diseases that you must be aware of as a landowner are as follows.

Fowl Cholera

A potentially fatal infectious illness, this type of cholera predominantly affects roosters during their later years. The most common signs and symptoms that you should look out for include diarrhea with a greenish hue, swollen joints, and a drop in the amount of feed that your chickens consume.

Coccidiosis

An infection that affects the digestive system, coccidiosis, is caused by ingesting contaminated food. Chickens affected by this illness may experience diarrhea, a gradual reduction in appetite, and a loss of body weight.

Avian Influenza

This disease is transmitted between birds of different species, particularly between aquatic wild creatures and chickens. The symptoms of the illness, which can prove to be fatal, include but are not limited to coughing, sneezing, swelling, awkward body discolorations, and changes in the appearance of chicken feathers.

Fowl Pox

Similar to chickenpox in humans, birds infected with fowl pox experience tiny eruptions on the surface of their skin. The disease is highly transmissible, and therefore, you may need to temporarily isolate the chicks that are suffering from the ailment from the rest of the flock.

Newcastle Disease

A potentially severe illness, Newcastle disease can adversely affect either your chickens' digestive, respiratory, or nervous systems. If you detect unusual eating habits, breathing patterns, or behaviors in any of your birds, it's important to get them tested, and if found to be infected, then treated for Newcastle disease.

Salmonellosis

A rare bacterial infection, the disease predominantly affects chickens during their primitive years. Rodents are the main carriers of the pathogen, and the symptoms of the illness can range from docile behavior to a change in the physiological appearance of the birds. Salmonellosis is relatively mild and rarely fatal.

Infectious Bronchitis

The disease is characterized by symptoms like coughing, sneezing, and a loss of appetite. It affects the respiratory system of the birds, and its causes and treatment are similar to the common flu in humans.

Marek's Disease

The prognosis of this illness in birds is rather debilitating, as nearly all the chickens that contract this disease eventually die. It is a viral infection that causes symptoms like depression and paralysis before it drives the birds to a painful end.

Parasitic Diseases

Parasites like worms and ticks are the most common causes of this group of illnesses in chickens. Infected birds may experience a loss of feathers and appetite, among other symptoms. Monitor for the presence of ticks by lifting the chicken's wings and looking for tiny dark specs – tick larvae. If you notice bloody diarrhea, it could be an indication of worms. Loss of weight, a decrease in activity, and a decline in egg production are other signs to look out for in parasitic infections.

Simple Remedies for Common Problems

While it is true that chickens are susceptible to a number of ailments, there are fortunately a handful of trivial, non-medicinal tricks that work well to cure sick birds. Most illnesses, particularly those that aren't fatal, tend to improve with a change in their diet. Adding more calcium to improve the egg laying capacity of non-fertile hens or including more protein in the daily ration to stimulate the growth of healthy microbes in diseased birds are classic examples of organic remedies. Nutrient supplements can also be used to correct metabolic and behavioral malfunctions. Herbs like thyme, rosemary, and turmeric are excellent for infectious diseases. Dried garlic is another organic ingredient that can help improve the health of fragile and sick chicks. These supplements can be mixed with the birds' feed to facilitate easy consumption and digestion. A few drops of apple cider vinegar in their drinking water can help resolve most gut-related issues in the birds. It is critical to note that natural health fixes take time to work, and therefore you will need to persist with them for at least a month, depending on the severity of the illness. As a poultry owner, however, you must remain open to other treatment options for your birds, such as medications, in the event that home remedies prove to be ineffective.

When Should You Worry About Your Chickens?

Cold weather exposure at temperatures beyond what the birds can comfortably tolerate is perhaps the aspect of raising chickens that needs your greatest attention. It is important to notice the signs of freezing in your birds and to take proactive steps to transfer them to a warmer site on your farm. Some chicken breeds are naturally more resistant to cold than others, and therefore it's best to look out for the physical manifestations of frostbite, like trembling, paralysis, changes in the color of the skin, ruffling of the feathers, and so on, to establish if a given temperature might be too cold for your birds. Chickens are hardy creatures, and they do not often display symptoms of illnesses until the disease has progressed to a later stage. There are, however, a number of minor physiological changes that you can keep an eye out for as a poultry owner. This will help you become aware of the struggles of your birds sooner and address their problems before things spiral out of control. Chicken droppings usually provide the first signs of internal malfunctions. Unusual color and texture may indicate an underlying illness related to the birds' digestive tract. Keeping an eye out for the body weight of mature chickens is another useful practice to detect diseases at an early stage. Unexplained weight loss or disproportionate weight gain are generally the symptoms of metabolic or infectious ailments. The external manifestations of fowl pox normally appear on the chicken's comb and wattles. These parts of a bird's physiological anatomy can also indicate frostbite or other injuries. Pale, bruised, or purple comb and wattles are the warning signs to pay attention to in this aspect. The eyes of a healthy chicken are clear, sensitive to light, and free of discharge. Abnormal changes in the form of swelling indicate infections. Nostrils without blockages and a smooth beak are indicators of good health in chickens. Noisy breathing and discharge from the mouth of a chicken are both early signs of a viral digestive or respiratory infection. Its feathers and skin also hold clues about potentially life-threatening illnesses. The feathers of the birds are naturally glossy, and they do not rise too much above the surface of the skin. Any changes to this normal texture is a worrying sign that you should not ignore. The skin of a chicken is not always visible, as it is entirely covered by feathers; you must, however, make it a routine practice to check the skin of your birds at least once a month. If you find abnormal aberrations, discolorations, or other unexplained alterations to the skin during your physical examination, you must have your bird evaluated by a medical practitioner. Healthy hens will lay eggs consistently, and they will have a firm breast. The keel, or the bone that runs down a chicken's body from between its breasts, should feel stiff to the touch. The crop and the abdomen may be slightly inflamed after a meal, but they should remain compressed and neither too hard nor too soft at all other times. Abnormalities on the feet, such as swelling of the scales, cuts, bruises, or lesions, are easy to notice. The root cause of these symptoms must be identified and treated promptly. Parasites like ticks very easily find their way to the area under a chicken's wings. Once there, they can cause severe sickness in your birds, so it is important to check your flock regularly. The bones on the wings must be firm, smooth, and injury-free. The glands and vents that are found on a chicken's body must not be overly dry or show signs of abnormalities in the form of bleeding.

CHICKEN ESSENTIALS

There are a few basic requirements that you will have to provide for in order to raise a happy flock. The succeeding paragraph briefly examines these indispensable needs.

Food: Just like every other living being, food is imperative for chickens. You must ensure that your feed is adequate, nutritious, fresh, and organic. Occasional treats are necessary to keep your birds in good health, but overdoing it can have negative repercussions.

Water: Another must for a chicken, providing clean drinking water for your birds at all times is important for their survival. Chickens might need more of it during the summer than during the winter. It is vital to pay attention to the temperature of the water during the colder months.

Shelter: When allowed to free range, chickens find their own shelters beneath bushes or trees. This clearly demonstrates their desire to have a roof over their heads. A coop is necessary for the birds to grow and develop freely. Maintaining the shelter through healthy sanitation practices is also vital.

Predator protection: Chickens are fragile birds, and they will need to be safeguarded from invaders. Having a strong biosecurity plan in place is mandatory to sustain your attempt at self-sustenance with poultry in the long-run.

Entertainment: Chickens are naturally mobile creatures, and they need space to run around and keep themselves entertained. Dust bathing is an activity that provides great pleasure to the birds, and hence you should set aside an area for the purpose on your farm or in your backyard. Reducing tension will also help to keep the birds happy and healthy. Provide enough room, food, and water to prevent the birds from quarreling with one another. Keep rooster numbers at a minimum and consider doing away with the more aggressive ones if they do no more than create or add to the nuisance in your flock.

Understand your birds: A successful mother hen is one who is aware of the needs of her flock. Spending time with your chickens and examining them while they wander about feeding, running, dust bathing, or mating will help you build an emotional connection with them. Once established, this bond will create in you the instinct that you need to truly understand what your birds require at any given point.

RAISING CHICKS

Leading a self-sufficient life brings with it the thrill of hatching your own eggs and caring for baby chicks until they mature into adult birds. The paragraphs that follow delve deeper into this aspect of managing a flock of hens and roosters.

Collecting Eggs

This part of poultry management is not only necessary to ensure the continuity of your flock, but it is also a fun practice to undertake. Providing nesting boxes for your hens will make it easy to locate the eggs once they are laid. Lining the bottom of these boxes with soft materials like straw will prevent the eggs from getting damaged. It's best practice to collect the eggs on the same day that your hens lay them. Doing so will not only mean that you have a basket of fresh eggs to consume, but it will also protect your produce from spoilage or damage. Chickens can sometimes crack or eat their own eggs, and they might also occasionally stain them with their poop. Picking the eggs soon after they are laid will help to prevent these possibilities from occurring. It is vital to ensure that your hands are clean and sanitized before you collect the eggs from the nesting boxes. These eggs can be wiped dry or washed with warm water if necessary before they are transferred to an incubator to go through the process of hatching into baby chicks, or stored in a refrigerator until they're ready for consumption.

Hatching Eggs

You could use the eggs that your hens lay, or you could order a handful from a hatchery to experience the joy of seeing little chicks come to life. Eggs can be hatched either naturally by the mother hen herself or artificially by placing them in an incubator. Both processes will yield the desired result only if the eggs are fertile, that is, if they are the result of mating between a hen and a rooster. So, if you don't have a rooster in your flock, then don't expect to have any fertile eggs. You'll want to be able to differentiate a fertile egg from an infertile one to know which eggs to store and which ones to place in the incubator if you choose to hatch them. The best way to tell a fertile egg from an infertile egg is through the candling method. You'll need to start by incubating the egg for a week. Once those 7 days are up, you'll remove the egg from the incubator (for no longer than 30 minutes) and shine a bright light, such as a flashlight or candle, through the egg in a dark room. This process illuminates the inside of the egg to allow you to check for any structures that would indicate a fertile egg, such as blood vessels, which will appear as dark lines, or a small, dark shape in the center, which is the embryo. If the egg lacks either of these things and looks clear, then your egg is infertile and should be discarded.

For the fertile eggs, a simulated environment that attempts to replicate the temperature and humidity that are created when a hen sits on her eggs to fertilize them is known as hatching by incubation. The ideal temperature for chickens is between 99 °F and 102 °F, with an optimum temporary heat level of 105 °F at certain stages. It takes on average 21 days for baby chicks to appear, and all you will need to do in those days is regulate the temperature, maintain the humidity, and rotate the eggs every now and then if you are using a manual incubator. You must refrain from opening the incubator, unless really necessary, during the 21-day period. This will prevent unnecessary loss of heat and help retain the required temperature on the inside. Observing the eggs through candling for not more than three minutes outside the incubator at any given time, can reveal damages to, or the death of, the embryo. It can sometimes take a little more than 21 days for your eggs to hatch, and once the little ones break out of the shell, they must be moved to a brooder for growth and nourishment.

Caring for Baby Chicks

Once you hear the squeak of the little chicks, it's important to move the tiny creatures to a preheated brooder. You must ensure that the brooder is well prepared at least 48 hours before the arrival of the baby chicks. It must be spacious enough to allow sufficient room for each chick. You may have to invest in a heating lamp to keep the birds warm inside the brooder. Additionally, wooden bedding arrangements must be made for the little chicks to rest on. The young creatures will usually need to remain in the brooder for about eight weeks, or until they are large enough to be moved into a coop. As a poultry owner hatching your own eggs, you will need to teach your chicks to eat and drink after they are born. Water can be introduced almost immediately, and by guiding one baby chick to the source, you should be able to train the entire flock to hydrate themselves. About four to six hours after hatching, starter feed can be offered to the young birds. Continue this diet until the chicks are about eight weeks old before you transition to other feeds specific to mature birds. Remember to adjust the feed based on the level of growth of your chicks and to gradually reduce the temperature within the brooder as the birds adapt to their new environment. Move the chickens to a coop once they outgrow the space they have in the brooder.

CHAPTER SUMMARY

- Understanding what your chickens need to survive happily is crucial to sustaining poultry over a period of time.

- What you feed your birds and how you manage their illnesses are vital parts of poultry keeping.
- Food, water, shelter, entertainment, predator protection, and your time are what a flock of hens and roosters requires to thrive.

6

FEATHER DUSTING YOUR COOP

Of all the tasks that you need to undertake to manage your flock in your backyard, keeping their shelter tidy is perhaps the most paramount. A clean coop can keep your birds healthy, as the chances of contracting illnesses in a neat environment are extremely small. As you develop the habit of clearing the trash from the chicken shelter regularly, you will find that your coop no longer emits a disturbing smell and that your farm is free of pest infestations altogether. The quality of the eggs that you consume from your backyard will also be enhanced when they are laid in a tidy environment. For all these reasons, it is vital to maintain a clean coop at all times.

PREPARING TO CLEAN YOUR COOP

When you have a large chicken shelter or a very small but messy one, tidying it up can seem like a daunting task. Yet, with the right supplies in hand, the process will not be complex in the least. Below are some of the essentials that you'll need for cleaning your chicken shelter.

Personal Supplies

While a dirty coop can become the root cause of a host of illnesses in your flock, exposing yourself to such a shelter without personal protection can be dangerous for your own well-being. Consequently, when you prepare yourself to deep clean or routinely scrub the dirt off your coop, it is vital to procure a pair of tight-fitting rubber boots, gloves, and a face mask. Remember to wear full clothing and refrain from handling chicken poop or other waste with your bare hands. You could use protective eyeglasses for greater safety, and you must always remember to discard the accessories that you use during cleaning. Certain pathogens, like salmonella, can be transmitted to humans from poultry and cause severe illness. Therefore, staying safe as a chicken owner yourself is vital to ensuring your well-being.

Cleaning Supplies

Gathering the things that you will need to tidy up your shelter is the next step in cleaning your coop. Mud and other dry debris can be removed using a cleaning brush or a rake. You should consider investing in a litter scoop to make your life easier when cleaning out your coop, as it'll help remove all the bird droppings. You'll likely need varying sizes of scrub brushes to remove the waste from the remote corners of your shelter. A soft cloth or dry sponge is useful to wipe the surfaces of electrical fittings like heating lamps. It's always wise to have a broom, a mop, and a bucket close at hand while tidying up your bird shelter. Keep a water hose handy when deep cleaning the chicken aboard. Liquid soap or other organic cleaning agents are also needed for the process. A common and very easy cleaning solution you can make at home is a simple mixture of distilled white vinegar and water. Take a spray bottle and mix one part vinegar with one part water, and voila! You now have yourself an excellent cleaning solution for your coop.

Other Supplies

If you intend to change the bedding, the nesting boxes, or any other accessories within the coop, you will need fresh bedding ready to replace the soiled bedding after cleaning. A trash bin to collect the litter from the coop is paramount. If your farm is large or if the pile of debris is too much to carry around in a dustbin, you could consider investing in a wheelbarrow to move the waste more conveniently across your land.

Managing Chickens During Cleaning

Before you enter the shelter with your protective gear, cleaning, and other supplies, you'll want to guide the flock out of the coop. You could move the birds to a part of the shelter that you aren't cleaning if the area is large enough, or you could simply engage them in an outdoor activity on your farm. Cleaning the coop at a time when the chickens naturally make their way out into the wild is a useful tip to carry out the task without interference from your birds. Remember to practice safety and hygiene measures if you are forced to physically handle the chickens that you can't temporarily remove from the coop. Choosing a bright, sunny day to clean the shelter will not only be beneficial for the process itself, but it will also make it easy to engage your birds in the outdoors.

STEP-BY-STEP GUIDE TO DEEP CLEANING YOUR COOP

A healthy habit to cultivate as a poultry owner is to remove waste like chicken droppings from the coop on a daily basis. Remember to change your clothes, gloves, and shoes after tidying up the shelter and before you handle the produce of the birds. While this daily practice is not time-consuming, deep cleaning your shelter can be a more cumbersome exercise. The steps that are outlined below will greatly simplify the task.

Step one: Empty the shelter completely. Guide the flock out of the coop and remove everything from the bedding to the nesting boxes, feeders, and waterers.

Step two: Use a rake, brush, or a stainless steel scraper to remove dry debris from the coop. Sweeping the floor is optional, but you could consider using the ploy if you find that your shelter has large amounts of accumulated dust piles in the corners or on the surfaces of coop accessories like lamps and roosts.

Step three: Look for structural damages in the shelter and fix them as needed. Patch up any holes with wood pieces to prevent those tiny rodents from invading your flocks' home.

Step four: Prepare the shelter for wet cleaning by cutting off the electricity supply. Dissolve the cleaning agent of your choice in water and soak every part of the coop with the liquid. Thoroughly scrub the dirty areas of the shelter. If you have a powerwasher this would be a great time to pull it out. However, a regular garden hose with a spray nozzle will suffice. Spray down the inside of the coop starting from top to bottom to clear any remaining debris your rakes and brushes couldn't reach. Wipe the coop clean with clean rags or paper towels.

Step five: Use a disinfectant on the inside of the coop and sanitize every poultry accessory.

Step six: Allow the coop to dry, preferably in sunlight. You could use a blower or a fan if the weather in your region is damp or too cold to facilitate natural drying.

Step seven: Once dry, add fresh bedding to the coop, about 6 inches high. You can use pine shavings and straw for the base layer and add bedding on top. Allow your chickens to wander back into the coop and repeat the deep cleaning process once every six months or as and when required.

Step eight: Dispose of the waste that you collected from the chicken shelter in a manner that suits your individual circumstances. Chicken poop can be incinerated or turned into garden compost with other waste like worn-out bedding.

Tips for Preventing a Stinky Coop

While the act of extensively cleaning your chicken shelter is performed twice a year, there are many more healthy practices that you can incorporate into your daily schedule to maintain a tidier coop. Not allowing chicken poop or waste to accumulate inside the shelter is a useful tip to consider. Use your litter scoop to remove the chicken poop if you notice it start to pile up. A well-ventilated coop is better for your birds as well as for you. Open the windows of your chicken shelter or use artificial means, like a fan, to circulate the air on the inside. The blowing breeze will help reduce the unpleasant odor of poultry waste. Another handy tip to maintain a fresh smell in your chicken shelter is to make use of strong herbs like mint or oregano. Adding these sporadically to your bedding will aid sanitation as well as smell. Dry spaces generally do not emit foul smells or attract pathogens. Making an attempt to prevent puddles of water from forming inside your coop, as well as to reduce the moisture content on the inside, are healthy practices in this regard. In spite of these efforts, if you find it difficult to manage poultry odor in your coop, you could opt for an enzymatic treatment to decompose the poop of your birds. You will likely require the assistance of a certified medical professional to implement this course of action. Utilizing sand wherever possible, particularly on the run, can make it easy to break down waste in a biologically friendly manner. A large amount of the poultry trash that you will need to clear from your coop on a daily basis will comprise chicken feces. To simplify the rather difficult task of scooping the poop from the floor of your shelter, you could use one of the following tips.

Dropping trays: Installing these in the coop can make it easy to clear the poop as the waste remains concentrated on designated boards. All you will need to do is clean the trays and place them back in the shelter.

Deep layers: If you do not particularly enjoy scooping the poop of your birds, you can choose this alternative to manage poultry waste. I personally don't use this method as I can't stand leaving bird feces in my coop for that long. But should you choose this route, you must do it correctly. For a general review of deep layering, you'll need to create a thick layer of the material of your choice for the floor of the coop. Make sure to select a substance that absorbs ammonia and nitrogen, both of which are key components of chicken feces. It's recommended to start with a base layer of pine shavings 4-6 inches deep, followed with leaves and grass clippings. The depth of the bedding will mean that the poop of the birds seeps downward, where it will disintegrate into compost. In this way, you will not have to clear the natural waste of your birds, and you will also have a pile of fresh manure that you can use elsewhere on your farm.

Tarp sheet: For this method, you cover the floor of your coop with a tarp. All kinds of poultry debris will accumulate on the sheet, and you can simply discard it and replace it with a fresh one when it gets too dirty. Alternatively, you could give the sheet a wet wash and restore it on the floor of your coop once it is dry. Cleaning a tarp is much easier than tidying up an entire coop.

SPACE AND SAFETY

Every bird needs adequate personal space within the coop. To promote a sense of happy coexistence among your birds, it is important to provide each one of them with separate bedding and sufficient surrounding space. The shelter must also comprise a designated area for nesting and roosting. The safety of your chickens is not only concerned with keeping predators away, but it also entails ensuring a secure atmosphere within the shelter. This can be achieved through proper ventilation and lighting. When using heat lamps, it's important to get them installed by a professional, as this will minimize the chances of electrical accidents in the form of short circuits or fires in the coop.

MAINTENANCE

There are a number of facets to keeping your birds' shelter neat and tidy. Firstly, you must ensure that the coop and the areas around it are not clogged up with unnecessary waste or poultry dust. It is a healthy practice to change chicken bedding every few weeks, as not doing so can make it difficult to clean up the poop buildup in the shelter. The nesting boxes must be free of dust, and the water containers must be washed thoroughly to prevent the spread of infections from contamination in your flock. Checking the feeder and removing the unconsumed food can help you better maintain your coop. Remember to look for holes, cracks, or loose ends in the structure of your chicken shelter every now and then. Fixing these is crucial to keeping predators away as well as preventing germs and other pathogens from entering the coop and making your birds sick. Staying vigilant about potential signs and symptoms of underlying medical conditions in your chickens is equally important. Make it a part of your maintenance routine to physically evaluate your birds at least once every 30 days, raise any alarming findings with your medical practitioner, and pursue the best course of action based on the illness. Besides making arrangements for proper circulation of air in the coop, you must ensure that your chicken shelter receives adequate sunlight for at least a few hours during the day. This will keep the internal environment of the chicken aboard dry and free of microbes. There must, however, also be spaces within the shelter that allow the birds to unwind in the shade when it gets too hot inside. Since chickens require a separate dust bathing area within the shelter, the coop can get extremely dirty. It is therefore a good idea to deep clean the shelter once in a while. Attempt to stay away from chemicals or other harsh cleaning agents and adopt organic ones to tidy up your coop.

CHECKLIST FOR CARING FOR YOUR CHICKENS

The following are the activities that you would need to undertake in the time specified to keep your flock happy and healthy.

Daily

- Thoroughly wash the water containers and refill them with fresh water.
- Feed your birds at fixed time intervals.
- Collect the eggs while they are fresh.
- Spend time with your birds with the intention of understanding their needs.

Monthly

- Change the bedding.
- Clean the nesting boxes thoroughly. Replace the material on the floor of the boxes as and when needed, particularly when the hens crack their own eggs and release the yolk.
- Sanitize the watering containers.
- Examine your birds to detect any physiological symptoms of poultry illnesses.

Biannually

- Deep clean every part of the coop.
- Make seasonal changes to your poultry infrastructure as applicable.

PROTECTING YOUR GARDEN FROM CHICKENS

Having a lush space with fruits and vegetables on your farm can be tricky if you don't take sufficient measures to safeguard it from chickens. The birds are experts at picking away at loose soil, and they might indulge in your berries and squash, so much so that you have nothing left for your household. Fortunately, however, there are a number of simple changes that you can make to the landscape of your farm to ensure that both your poultry and garden vegetation thrive peacefully side-by-side. Fencing the plants that you want to keep chickens away from is a useful technique. You could choose one of the many materials for fencing that were discussed earlier. If your birds are larger and tend to fly over the fencing protection, you could employ a hardware cloth to deter them from venturing into the region. Weeds also work well to keep your strawberries out of reach of the little creatures. There are not many coexistence problems on a farm that cannot be solved by a ring of stones or bricks. Surrounding the plants that you want to protect will drive chickens away relatively easily. Also, making sure that your birds have sufficient space to wander about during the daytime, and enough food to satisfy their hunger, will keep them away from your garden naturally. You could also consider planting shrubs or bushes exclusively for your birds to discourage them from moving into your garden.

Pro Tips

A few more tricks that you could use to deter chickens from spoiling your garden are:

- Surround your vegetation with chicken wire.

- Use citrus peels or juices along the rim of your garden to keep the birds at bay, as they despise the strong citrus smell.
- Cultivate herbs that chickens naturally dislike, such as lavender, catnip, peppermint, and chives, alongside your preferred fruit and vegetable crops.
- Use fear-triggering symbols like a scarecrow to keep your garden safe.
- Pets like dogs can be trained to watch over your plantation and keep the birds away.

UNDERSTANDING NORMAL CHICKEN BEHAVIORS

There are certain personality characteristics and instinctive behaviors that are inherent in chickens. As a poultry owner, you must never attempt to suppress or alter them. Becoming aware of what is and isn't natural in the birds will help you sustain a happy and healthy flock.

Mating

This behavior pattern is only applicable to flocks that comprise both hens and roosters. Similar to humans, the female chicks choose their preferred mating partner. A rooster will gather some food and attempt to capture the attention of the hens in the flock through verbal sounds. Once one or more of the birds are sufficiently attracted, the rooster will perform a chicken dance, which involves a flapping of the wings and revolving around the hens. The female bird will generally express her approval by squatting before the rooster. The mating attempt fails if the hen walks away from the site.

Preening

Chickens generally like to undertake this activity in groups. During preening, a chicken attempts to correctly align its feathers using its beak. In most cases, it will follow this up by stimulating the gland situated on the edge of its tail. The oil that is released as a result is applied all over its feather coat. This kind of preening behavior is normal and even necessary for your birds, as the feathers are more than just ornamental in chickens. They perform important metabolic functions, like regulating the body temperature of the birds during the winter.

Dust Bathing

Chickens normally take a dust bath to not only clean their feathers but also to amuse themselves. If you have a designated dust bathing area in your coop, you will find that your birds often toss, roll, and jump in it.

Alternatively, the chickens will create their own dust bath by digging the land if you do not provide them with one. This shows that the practice is inherent in the birds.

Scratching

Another common habit among chickens is scratching the ground in search of food or to build a comfortable nest, an activity that your flock will certainly engage in. It is just as normal for the birds to peck at unusual objects on the ground or even in water.

Wandering

If you keep your birds confined to their shelter, you will soon discover that they force their way out of the coop and escape into the wild. This is because roaming about the fields is a behavioral pattern that helps chickens survive. They use the time away from the flock to de-stress, explore, and derive thrill from new adventures.

Pecking

Chickens within a flock establish their own social hierarchy. The most powerful bird becomes the leader of the pack, while the more fragile creatures drift to the bottom of the order. Chickens have the natural tendency to peck at one another, and they do so in accordance with the said structure. That is, a bird will only peck at those below it in the social order. Quarrels between roosters to move up the hierarchy are common among chickens. Other than pecking, a race to ascend to the top of the order can involve pushing, bumping, or other forced physical actions.

Brooding

Perhaps not all, but a few hens display brooding during the laying season. It's a behavior characterized by a sense of obsessive protectiveness toward its own eggs. Such hens attempt frantically to hatch baby chicks even out of infertile eggs. Collecting the produce of such mother hens can be challenging, and you may have to confront violent reactions from the bird if you try to get close to her eggs. Brooding is caused by a hormonal imbalance in the chicken, and it can often be corrected by cutting down on the amount of calcium and protein that you feed the bird.

CHAPTER SUMMARY

- Maintaining a clean coop has a plethora of advantages both for your flock and for your self-sustenance attempt.
- Emptying the coop, dry cleaning the interiors, washing the floor, the walls, and the ceiling, and

replacing the shelter with new poultry accessories are steps involved in tidying up your chicken aboard.

- Dust bathing, scratching, preening, pecking, brooding, and mating are behaviors natural to chickens.

7

BREAKING SOME EGGS

As a rich source of animal protein, chicken is not only delicious to eat, but it is also extremely beneficial for your overall health. It helps to prevent obesity and slow down the age-related weakening of your bones and muscles. When consumed in the recommended quantities, chicken meat can promote cardiovascular health. It's abundant in micronutrients, vitamin B12, and other essential minerals. Chicken eggs are an equally powerful source of calcium, protein, phosphorus, and unsaturated fats. Eggs can help to keep your blood pressure in check, increase the good cholesterol levels in your body, and strengthen your bones and joints. The sense of satisfaction that you feel when you consume an egg, knowing that it is good for your system, is all the more amplified when it comes straight from your backyard. This is because with chickens, the quality of the produce is directly dependent on what is fed to the birds. As a poultry owner, you can control what your hens eat, and you can be assured that your eggs contain every nutrient that you want them to have. When you pick your eggs daily, there can be no question of spoilage or a lack of freshness in the food that you consume. Above all, it provides the opportunity to indulge in your favorite meat without worrying about the manner in which the birds may have been treated in slaughterhouses before they were culled. It has been scientifically proven that eggs, when consumed fresh, have a greater nutritional content and color when compared to store-bought ones. Utilizing the eggs and meat from your own birds produces a level of satisfaction that cannot be matched by purchasing supplies from the grocery store.

THE EGGS METHOD FOR BOOSTING YOUR EGG PRODUCTION

The **EGGS** approach is a useful technique to ensure that you have a basket full of fresh eggs to consume as a family each week. The steps involved in the method are:

Evaluate your goals: Long before you bring home a flock of chickens, it's important to define your objective for adopting the path of self-sustenance. Do you require homegrown eggs for personal consumption? Or do you intend to make profits from their sale? How many eggs does your family ordinarily need on a weekly basis? Understanding your purpose will help you achieve the highest possible yield from your birds.

Gather the supplies: Preparing yourself to introduce chickens to your land is the next crucial step. You must put together everything that your birds will need for their growth. This includes a shelter, the correct type of feed, nesting boxes, a dust bathing area, roosts, and a water supply, amongst other essentials that were discussed earlier.

Get your chickens: The question of which breed might be right for you will depend on your objective as evaluated in step one and your poultry infrastructure as understood in step two. Different types of chickens have varying capacities to lay eggs, and they have marginally differing needs for their sustenance. You must be careful to choose the type of chicken that fits both of the above parameters in your case.

Sustainably manage waste: Optimal handling of poultry debris is paramount to ensuring a happy and healthy flock. You can choose one of the many methods of waste disposal that were discussed earlier. When your hens are stress- and disease-free, they will lay eggs consistently all through the year. Once you implement the EGGS method for improving the output of your female birds, you will be able to regularly pick fresh and nutritious eggs.

WHY IS YOUR EGG PRODUCTION GOING DOWN?

Coming to the realization that the hens in your backyard aren't laying as many eggs as the other birds in the breed typically do can be stressful. Experiencing a sudden drop in the quantity of the produce of your flock can be just as nerve racking. Becoming aware of the many causes that can lead to a decline in egg productivity in your hens can help you better manage and overcome the situation when it arises.

Food: Inadequate food can adversely affect the number of eggs your hens lay. Likewise, the absence of essential nutrients in their feed can also cause a long-term decline in productivity.

Water: If your birds are denied access to clean drinking water, they will not lay eggs as frequently as they should. With chickens, even a few hours of water deprivation can cause severe disturbances to the reproductive cycle.

Stress: This is one of the main causes for a drop in egg production in chickens. The birds can be stressed for a host of reasons, among them a lack of harmony in the flock, insufficient room within the coop and outside, not being able to unwind or wander about freely, and fear of predators.

Illness: You can expect to collect fewer eggs from hens that are sick. Besides viral or bacterial infections, diseases caused by pests like ticks and mice can also lead to a drop in fertility.

Biological factors: As your hens age, the number of eggs they lay will decrease. Certain kinds of genetic mutations that affect the reproductive tract can also cause a decline in the volume of the produce of your flock.

External causes: Many times, environmental factors like extreme weather conditions are behind the drop in egg production of your hens. A large number of broody hens in your flock can also create a tendency in your birds to focus more on hatching than on laying fresh eggs. Inadequate daylight during the winter days also contributes to a decline in the volume of eggs.

HOW TO BOOST EGG PRODUCTION

There is no need to be overly concerned when you discover that your hens aren't as productive as they were before, or as they should be. This is because there are a number of easy fixes that you could implement within your flock to boost the volume of eggs. The steps that you can take aside from selecting a breed that is known for its egg-laying capacity are discussed below.

Nutritional Remedies

Feeding your birds a balanced diet usually solves the problem of infertility in a reasonably short time. Egg-laying hens require a feed that is rich in protein and calcium. Other foods that are known to stimulate the reproductive system of the birds to produce a greater number of eggs include dried peppermint, fresh lemon, and moringa leaves. Administering these in addition to the regular chicken feed works well to improve fertility in hens. Adding a small amount of baking soda to the drinking water of your birds can also help the cause.

Supplementary Remedies

Calcium, protein, and chelated minerals, when given as supplements, improve the volume of egg production greatly. Probiotics have also been known to create the same positive impact in the birds, except that they work by improving the digestive health of the hens as opposed to regulating their reproductive cycles.

Lifestyle Remedies

When hens have adequate space, are exposed to sufficient natural or artificial light, and are stress-free, they tend to lay eggs consistently year-round. Moreover, a healthy flock is always more productive than a group of sick hens. Therefore, it is crucial to pay attention to the well-being of your birds. Placing nesting boxes sporadically all around the coop will promote an egg-laying culture among your female birds. Hens prefer to lay eggs in clean surroundings, so you'll only benefit from keeping their shelter and your farm tidy. It's always best to attempt to improve the egg production of your flock through the above-mentioned natural remedies before experimenting with other non-organic solutions.

HOW TO RAISE CHICKENS FOR MEAT?

While the basics of raising chickens for laying eggs or for meat are more or less the same, there are certain special considerations that you need to keep in mind while maintaining a flock for meat.

Breed type: The Cornish Cross, Rhode Island Red, Buff Orpington, and Ranger breeds are ideal for use as meat birds. In a generic sense, all chicken varieties that tend to grow large in size can be raised for their meat. Dual purpose Heritage breeds work just as well in this aspect.

Time: The body weight of the birds is the most crucial measure when figuring out the right time to slaughter them. Different breeds have varying weight thresholds, and it's important to know the value that corresponds to your chicken type before you cull them for their meat. The most common meat variant, the Cornish Cross, attains the recommended weight in seven to nine weeks from birth. Other chickens, however, can be slaughtered up to the age of six months to be used as roasts or soup meats.

Feeding: The breeds that are maintained for meat tend to grow immensely in size even with a small amount of chicken feed. As a poultry owner, therefore, it's important for you to focus your attention on preventing overeating in your birds. Protein is the most essential component for the chickens to mature into a size that is ideal for butchering. It should make up at least 20% of the bird's diet for the first three weeks and a minimum of 18% thereafter. Access to clean drinking water is equally essential in this regard.

Shelter: The housing requirement of meat-producing chicken birds is similar to their egg-laying counterparts, with the only exception being that these birds might move out of a brooder and into a full-sized coop much sooner. You will need to make arrangements for chicken bedding that is made up of a highly porous material because meat chickens tend to poop more often and in greater quantities. It is vital to keep the coop clean to prevent the spread of diseases in your flock and the possibility of you consuming the meat of an infected bird.

Other factors: Many aspects of the life of a meat chicken can intimidate a new poultry owner, yet it is crucial that you stand by your objective behind adopting the path of self-sustenance. While it's important to look after your flock, it is perhaps more vital to refrain from establishing an emotional connection with the birds that you plan to slaughter for meat. This will make the processing and butchering of your chickens less challenging on a personal level.

HOW TO SLAUGHTER OR GET THE CHICKENS SLAUGHTERED?

If you wish to butcher your chicken in a processing unit, you can get in touch with one close to where you reside. The agency will likely arrange for trained individuals to visit your farm and hand pick the birds that are ready for slaughter. The culling process will be completed at a nearby commercial facility, and the meat from your flock will be ready for consumption in a matter of hours. This method of butchering is ideal if you want to sell the produce of your backyard birds. On the contrary, if you require the meat for your household, you could consider culling the birds yourself. The step-by-step process for the same is discussed below.

Slaughter Preparation

Begin by choosing the bird that is ready for butchering in terms of its age and body weight. Designate a separate area of your farm or backyard for the slaughter process. It is advisable to use the same space for all subsequent cullings. Remember to butcher no more than one chicken at a time. Gather the supplies that are paramount for slaughter. These include a couple of poultry knives, a killing cone, a scalding pot, a thermometer, a bucket, a dustbin, an empty container, a broomstick, and cleaning products as required.

Killing

Hold or suspend the selected bird upside down. Gain control over the living creature with the help of the killing cone. Grab the chicken by its head using the cone, and using a poultry knife, make a deep cut on the neck of the bird below its jaw. Tilt back the head of the dead chicken marginally and collect the oozing blood in a container. Stretch out its neck, and with your knife, separate the head from the rest of the body.

Scalding

Submerge the carcass in a scalding pot of warm water, the temperature of which must range between 135 °F and 170 °F. Allow the bird to remain underwater for approximately 45 seconds to 1 minute. You can check the readiness of the bird for the next step by pulling it out of the water and plucking a few feathers. If the skin tears easily then the water is too hot or the bird has been in the water too long. If the feathers don't come off easily then the water is either not hot enough or the chicken needs to be scalded for a bit longer.

Plucking

After the chicken has undergone scalding, you should be able to pick the feathers from its body relatively easily. Hold the chicken upside down by the legs and start plucking on the drumsticks and make your way down. Carry out this step with gentle hands, or you may risk damaging the skin of the bird. You could also use an electric feather picker instead of your hands to complete this part of the process.

Gutting

If you have someone in your community with experience in gutting, I strongly recommend watching them first, or even watching a video on the internet before tackling this step, as it can be tricky to grasp by just reading how to do it in text form. It's also important to familiarize yourself with a chicken's anatomy to better understand exactly what you're dealing with when gutting a chicken.

Start by laying the chicken on its back. Using your knife, cut off the feet at the joints. Make a cut through the skin of the bird, either from its top or rear end. Make a deeper insertion into the network of tissues and release the organs of the body. Removing one part is usually sufficient to strip the carcass of its entire contents.

Once the inside contents are sufficiently discarded, take your hose with a sprayer head on it and rinse the inside and outside of the bird.

Cooling

The chicken needs to cool before storing. Fill a large bucket or container with ice and water and submerge the chicken for anywhere between 6-24 hours.

STORING THE CHICKEN ONCE BUTCHERED

Follow the procedure outlined below to consume the meat from your backyard while it is fresh and free of microbes.

- Remove the chicken from the cold water and pat it dry.
- Wrap it in plastic paper and place it in the lower part of your refrigerator. The meat can also be stored in a container or on a refrigerator board. Ensure that the temperature of your refrigerator is 37 °F or lower.
- Consume raw poultry within 24 hours or, at the latest, within 48 hours from the time of its butchering.
- Remember to wash your hands and every kitchen appliance, container, countertop, and other equipment that was exposed to the raw meat with warm water and soap. Giving them a second rinse with diluted bleach is also a useful habit to cultivate.
- Cooked chicken can be stored in the refrigerator for no more than three to four days.

Pro tip: You could fix labels on your meat containers with the date on which they were butchered to help you keep track.

If you don't plan on consuming the chicken in the next couple days, you'll need to freeze it. I recommend vacuum sealing the bird to prevent freezer burn. Try to consume the meat within one year to not compromise quality.

CHAPTER SUMMARY

- The absence of essential nutrients like calcium and protein in the diet of the birds is one of the primary reasons for a drop in the volume of egg production.
- There are a number of non-organic techniques that can be used to ensure that your hens lay eggs consistently all year.
- You must pay special attention to the diet of your birds when you raise them for their meat.

CHICKEN BREED APPENDIX

Breed	Egg per annum	Egg Color	Egg size	Purpose
55 Flowery Hen	250–300	Cream	Large	Eggs
Ameraucana	250	Pale Blue	Large	Eggs
Ancona	220	White	Extra Large	Eggs
Andalusian	165	White	Large	Eggs
Araucana	250	Pale Blue	Large	Eggs
Australorp	250	Light brown	Large	Dual
Barnvelder	150–200	Dark brown	Large	Dual
Bielefelder	230	Brown with pink undertones	Large	Dual
Black Star/Red Star	300	Variable	Large	Dual
Brahma	150–200	Brown	Medium	Dual

Brakel	180–200	White	Large	Dual
Buckeye	150–200	Brown	Large	Dual
Buttercups	150–200	White	Medium	Eggs
Campine	150–200	White	Medium	Eggs
Chantecler	200	Brown	Large	Dual
Cinnamon Queen	250–300	Brown	Large	Eggs
Cochin	150–200	Brown	Small	Eggs
Cornish	-	-	-	Meat
Cream Legbar	160–200	Sky Blue/Pale Green	Small	Eggs
Delaware	208	Brown	Extra-large	Dual
Dominique	100–150	Brown	Large	Exhibit
Dorking	100–150	White	Medium	Dual
Easter Egger	280	Blue/Brown	Medium	Dual

Faverolle	100–150	Light Brown	Medium	Dual
Friesan	150–180	White	Small	Eggs
Gournay	150	White	Large	Dual
Hamburg	200	White	Medium	Eggs
Holland	250–300	White	Large	Dual
Isbar	200	Green	Large	Eggs
Java	150–200	Brown	Large	Eggs
Jersey Giant	260	Brown	Large	Dual
Leghorn	280–300	White	Extra Large	Eggs
Majorca	150–200	White	Large	Eggs
Maran	150–200	Chocolate Brown	Extra Large	Dual
Minocra	200–250	White	Extra Large	Eggs
Naked Neck	100–150	Brown	Large	Dual

New Hampshire Red	150–200	Brown	Extra large	Dual
Olive Egger	150–200	Green	Large	Dual
Orpington	200	Brown	Large	Dual
Plymouth Rock	250–300	Brown	Large	Dual
Polish	250–300	White	Medium	Eggs
RedCaps	150–200	White	Medium	Dual
Rhode Island Red	275–300	Brown	Large	Dual
Speckledy	250–270	Chestnut Brown	Medium	Dual
Sussex	250	Light Brown	Large	Dual
Welsummer	150–200	Dark Brown	Large	Eggs
Whiting True Blue	150–200	Blue	Medium	Eggs
Wyandotte	200	Light Brown	Large	Eggs

If you decide to use these plans, a variation of them, or make your own, I'd love to see the final product! Please consider sharing pictures of your finished coop in the review section of this book on Amazon so we can all bask in your hard work and success.

Chickens can primarily be classified into meat-producing, egg-laying, and hybrid breeds. While choosing a particular variety, it's important to evaluate your self-sustenance objectives in light of the characteristics of that very type. Understanding the costs associated with poultry farming is a crucial step in making the transition from a dependent lifestyle to an independent existence. There are a number of federal and state laws that pertain to the raising of chickens in backyards in America. A chicken coop is the most vital element of the poultry infrastructure that you need to set up on your land before you bring home a flock of hens and roosters. To be able to manage your birds well, it's crucial that you become aware of the type of food that they need, the kind of risk they face from predators, and the various diseases that they can potentially be infected with. Fertile eggs, when placed in an incubator, will hatch into baby chicks. These need to be moved to a brooder temporarily before they can settle into their coop. It's imperative to follow a hygiene maintenance schedule to keep your birds healthy and happy. Besides eggs, chickens can also be raised for their meat. Certain special considerations need to be kept in mind while managing a group of birds that you plan to slaughter.

The many aspects of poultry farming can seem overwhelming at first, but once you take the first step, you will find that the practice becomes easy and begins to come naturally to you. The thrill of raising the little creatures into large birds and consuming fresh eggs and meat from them is a proposition that is too difficult to let go of once adopted. Now that you are equipped with the knowledge you need to traverse the path of self-sustenance with confidence and success, all that is left is to put an end to procrastination and begin the most fruitful ride of your life. The journey toward independence is beyond expression, and once you take the plunge, you will never want to return to the black-and-white world of urban existence ever again.

Note from the author: I have shared my experience with poultry farming with you with the intention of enabling you to experience the joy that we felt in raising our own food source. I am a testament to the many rewards that this way of life holds, and I urge you to explore, experiment, and share your own unique journey with others. I wish you the best of luck for what lies ahead.

If this book has provided you with the knowledge that you need to undertake poultry farming, or if it has helped you raise happy, healthy, and highly productive hens in a clean environment, then kindly consider leaving a review on Amazon.

Thank you, and happy farming!

REFERENCES

Agriculture Marketing Service. (n.d.). *Import requirements - table eggs.* Agriculture Marketing Service. https://www.ams.usda.gov/services/imports-exports/table-eggs

Animal and Plant Health Inspection Service U.S. Department of Agriculture. (2020). *National poultry improvement plan (NPIP).* Animal and Plant Health Inspection Service U.S. Department of Agriculture. https://www.aphis.usda.gov/aphis/ourfocus/animal health/nvap/nvap-reference-guide/poultry/national-poultry-improvement-plan

Arcuri, L. (2023). *How to collect and clean chicken eggs.* The Spruce. https://www.thespruce.com/collect-clean-and-store-chicken-eggs-3016828

Arcuri, L. (2022). *How to take care of your chickens: A daily checklist.* The Spruce. https://www.thespruce.com/daily-and-monthly-chicken-care-tasks-3016823

Armitage, N. (2022). *When is the best time to buy chicks?* Cluckin. https://cluckin.net/when-is-the-best-time-to-buy-chicks.html

Backyard Chicken Chatter. (n.d.). *How to weatherproof a chicken coop – 6 steps to protect your flock.* Backyard Chicken Chatter. https://www.backyardchickenchatter.com/how-to-weatherproof-a-chicken-coop/

Bentoli. (n.d.). *6 common chicken problems you can eliminate with quality nutrients.* Bentoli. https://www.bentoli.com/chicken-problems-common/

BrainyQuote. (n.d.). *Chicken Quotes.* BrainyQuote. https://www.brainyquote.com/quotes/eartha_kitt_601670?src=t_chickens

California Department of Food and Agriculture. (n.d.). *Guidelines for poultry slaughter.* California Department of Food and Agriculture. https://www.cdfa.ca.gov/ahfss/mpes/pdfs/PoultryGuidelines.pdf

Connecticut Department of Agriculture. (n.d.). *Pet bird or poultry impor-*

tation permit. Connecticut Department of Agriculture. https://portal.ct.gov/DOAG/Regulatory/Regulatory/Pet-Bird-or-Poultry-Importation-Permit

Connecticut Department of Agriculture. (n.d.). *Poultry, intensive operation permit.*Connecticut Department of Agriculture. https://portal.ct.gov/DOAG/Commissioner/Commissioner/Poultry-Intensive-Operation-Permit

Connecticut Department of Agriculture. (n.d.). *Poultry Live Dealer's license.* Connecticut Department of Agriculture. https://portal.ct.gov/DOAG/Licensing/Licenses/Poultry-Live-Dealers-License

Coosemans, S. (n.d.). *Chickens and self-sufficiency: Is raising chickens cost-effective.* Sunny Simple Living. https://sunnysimpleliving.com/is-keeping-chickens-cost-effective/

Countryside. (2020). *5 Farm fresh egg benefits..* Countryside. https://backyardpoultry.iamcountryside.com/chickens-101/5-farm-fresh-egg-benefits/

Darre, M. (2014). *Cleaning and disinfecting your poultry house.* Cornell Small Farms. https://smallfarms.cornell.edu/2014/04/cleaning-and-disinfecting-your-poultry-house/

Douglas, J. (2021). *4 ways to start living self-sufficient lifestyle right now + why start ASAP.* Organic Growers School. https://organicgrowersschool.org/4-ways-to-start-living-self-sufficient-lifestyle-right-now-why-start-asap/

Eartheasy. (n.d.). *The complete guide to building a chicken coop.* Eartheasy. https://learn.eartheasy.com/guides/the-complete-guide-to-building-a-chicken-coop/

Eggshell. (2022). *Top 5 ways to make your chicken coop smell better.* Eggshell. https://www.eggshellonline.co.uk/top-5-ways-to-make-your-chicken-coop-smell-better

Erika. (n.d.). *How to live off the land? 31 things (2023) you should know.* Gokce Capital. https://gokcecapital.com/how-to-live-off-the-land/

Fewell, A. (2017). *8 common chicken illnesses & how to treat them.* The Fewell Homestead. https://thefewellhomestead.com/8-common-chicken-illnesses-how-to-treat-them/

Freeman, P. (2022). *Dos and don'ts when protecting chickens from predators.*

Countryside. https://backyardpoultry.iamcountryside.com/coops/protecting-chickens-from-predators/

Garman, J. (2022). *Dangers in the coop.* Countryside. https://backyardpoultry.iamcountryside.com/feed-health/dangers-in-the-coop/

Green America. (2022). *The many benefits of backyard chickens.* Green America. https://www.greenamerica.org/green-living/many-benefits-backyard-chickens#:~:text=As%20the%20Gidneys%20have%20learned,to%20local%2C%20sustainable%20food%20systems

Helpful-Twist7660. (2022). *Rules for starting your own poultry farm.* Reddit. https://www.reddit.com/r/TrendingInterior/comments/xr3e4s/rules_for_starting_your_own_poultry_farm/?utm_source=share&utm_medium=web2x&context=3

Hess, T & Griffler, M. (2018). *Daily diet, treats and supplements for chickens.* The Open Sanctuary Project, Inc. https://opensanctuary.org/chicken-diet-and-supplements/

Hudson, J. (2023). *14 chicken fencing ideas — Keep predators out.* Chicken Scratch. https://cs-tf.com/chicken-fence-ideas/

Hudson, J. (2022). *How cold is too cold for your chickens?.* Chicken Scratch. https://cs-tf.com/how-cold-is-too-cold-for-chickens/

Jacob, J, & Anderson, K. (n.d.). *Developing regulations for keeping urban chickens.* eXtension. https://poultry.extension.org/articles/poultry-management/urban-poultry/developing-regulations-for-keeping-urban-chickens/

Jacob, J. (n.d.). *Drugs approved for use in conventional poultry production.* eXtension. https://poultry.extension.org/articles/feeds-and-feeding-of-poultry/feed-additives-for-poultry/drugs-approved-for-use-in-conventional-poultry-production/

Jen. (2019). *What you should not feed your chickens.* Dine a Chook. https://www.dineachook.com.au/blog/what-you-should-not-feed-your-chickens/

Justin. (2015). *How to keep chickens happy and healthy with these 7 essential tips.* . https://abundantpermaculture.com/7-essentials-chicken-flock-alive-happy/

Keck Medicine of University of South California. (2022). *9 health benefits of eating eggs for breakfast.* Keck Medicine of University of South

California. https://www.keckmedicine.org/blog/10-healthy-bene-fits-of-eating-eggs-for-breakfast/#:~:text="Eggs%20are%20a%20good%20source,at%20Keck%20Medicine%20of%20USC

Lapingcao, C. (2021). *Chicken processing 101: When to slaughter your chickens, steps, and equipment.* The Happy Chicken Coop. https://www.thehappychickencoop.com/chicken-processing-know-when-to-slaughter-your-chickens/

Lesley, C. (2022). *Common chicken health problems.* Almanac. https://www.almanac.com/common-chicken-health-problems

Lesley, C. (2022). *Why Your Chickens Do What They Do..* Almanac. https://www.almanac.com/chicken-behaviors-dust-bathing-mating-preening-and-more

Lewis, E. (2021). *How to clean a chicken coop.* Countryside. https://backyardpoultry.iamcountryside.com/coops/clean-a-chicken-coop/

MacLean, K. (n.d.). *Understanding local laws for raising backyard chickens.* Pete and Gerry's. https://peteandgerrys.com/blogs/field-notes/local-laws-for-raising-backyard-chickens

Maryland OneStop. (n.d.). *Selling live poultry or hatching eggs details.* Maryland OneStop. https://onestop.md.gov/licenses/selling-live-poultry-or-hatching-eggs-5d1540b054f24d03e9998239

Maryland Department of Agriculture. (2019). *2019 small and other poultry market policy.* Maryland Department of Agriculture. https://mda.maryland.gov/AnimalHealth/Documents/swap-meet-policy.pdf

MCguire, V. (2013). *How to chicken-proof your garden.* Modern Farmer. https://modernfarmer.com/2013/06/how-to-chicken-proof-your-garden/

Messing, L & Schweihofer, J. (n.d.). *Handling, using, and storing poultry.* Michigan State University. https://www.canr.msu.edu/uploads/resources/pdfs/mi_fresh_poultry.pdf

Mock, S. (2017). *Top 5 tips for keeping your chicken coop clean.* Purely Poultry Blog. https://www.purelypoultry.com/blog/top-tips-for-keeping-your-coop-clean/

Mormino, K.S. (n.d.). *Chicken checkup: DIY physical exam.* The Chicken

Chick. https://the-chicken-chick.com/chicken-checkup-diy-physical-exam/

Mormino, K.S. (2020). *9 reasons (and solutions) for egg production decline.* (n.d.) Hobby Farms. https://www.hobbyfarms.com/9-reasons-and-solutions-for-egg-production-decline/

MorningChores. (n.d.). *How to go about choosing the perfect chicken breeds for you.* MorningChores. https://morningchores.com/choosing-a-chicken-breed/#:~:text=Choosing%20a%20Chicken%20Breed%20Best,chickens

Moyle, J. (2022). *Exhibiting and registering your flock.* University of Maryland. https://extension.umd.edu/resource/exhibiting-and-registering-your-flock

Mundorf, D. (2023). *14 chicken coop plans perfect for big or small homesteads.* Bob Vila. https://www.bobvila.com/articles/chicken-coop-plans/

National Chicken Council. (n.d.). *Animal welfare for broiler chickens.* National Chicken Council. https://www.nationalchickencouncil.org/policy/animal-welfare/

Pennsylvania Department of Agriculture. (n.d.). *Livestock and poultry mortality disposal in Pennsylvania.* Pennsylvania Department of Agriculture. https://www.agriculture.pa.gov/Animals/AHDServices/Pages/Livestock-and-Poultry-Mortality-Disposal.aspx

Purina. (n.d.). *Hatching eggs at home: A 21-day guide for baby chicks.* Purina. https://www.purinamills.com/chicken-feed/education/detail/hatching-eggs-at-home-a-21-day-guide-for-baby-chicks

Purina. (n.d.). *Why homegrown eggs are better.* Purina. https://www.purinamills.com/chicken-feed/education/detail/why-homegrown-eggs-are-better

Rachael. (2021). *7 ways to increase egg production in older hens.* Dine a Chook. https://www.dineachook.com.au/blog/7-ways-to-increase-egg-production-in-older-hens/

Robert. (2022). *The cost of raising backyard chickens — Will you save money.* Coop Design Plans. https://coopdesignplans.com/cost-of-raising-chickens/

Schirtzinger, S. & McDermott, T. (2017) *Chicken breed selection.* The Ohio State University. https://ohioline.osu.edu/factsheet/anr-60

Satak, W. (n.d.). *Special poultry permit.* Washington State Department of Agriculture. https://agr.wa.gov/departments/food-safety/food-safety/special-poultry-permit

Sharma, J. (2020). *How to improve FCR and reduce feed cost of poultry.* Prudence Technology USA Inc. https://www.navfarm.com/blog/improve-fcr-feed-cost-poultry/

Star Milling Co. (n.d.). *Breeds of chickens.* Star Milling Co. https://starmilling.com/poultry-chicken-breeds/

Star Milling Co. (n.d.). *Caring for baby chicks: What to do once they arrive.* Star Milling Co. https://www.purinamills.com/chicken-feed/education/detail/caring-for-baby-chicks-what-to-do-once-they-arrive#:~:text=Introduce%20baby%20chicks%20to%20water,is%20essential%20for%20healthy%20chicks

Steele, L. (2023). *Best chicken breeds for eggs.* Almanac. https://www.almanac.com/raising-chickens-101-choosing-chicken-breeds

Talmage Farm Agway. (n.d.). *The importance of a chicken coop.* Talmage Farm Agway. https://talmagefarm.com/blog/48874/the-importance-of-a-chicken-coop

Tamil Nadu Agricultural University. (n.d.). *Biosecurity and disease management.* Tamil Nadu Agricultural University. https://agritech.tnau.ac.in/expert_system/poultry/Biosecurity%20and%20Disease%20Management.html

The Happy Chicken Coop. (2022). *Chicken fencing — Which one should you choose.* The Happy Chicken Coop. https://www.thehappychickencoop.com/chicken-fencing/

The Happy Chicken Coop. (2020). *How to raise meat chickens.* The Happy Chicken Coop. https://www.thehappychickencoop.com/how-to-raise-meat-chickens/

The Happy Chicken Coop. (2022). *The 7 best places to buy chickens.* The Happy Chicken Coop. https://www.thehappychickencoop.com/the-7-best-places-to-buy-chickens/

The Feather Brain. (n.d.). *When to buy baby chicks: The simple calculation to find which day is best for you.* The Feather Brain. https://www. thefeatherbrain.com/blog/when-to-buy-chicks

U.S. Food & Drug Administration. (2023). *Animal Drugs, Feeds, and Related Products.* U.S. Food & Drug Administration. https://www. accessdata.fda.gov/scripts/cdrh/cfdocs/cfcfr/CFRSearch.cfm? CFRPart=558&showFR=1

van Uitert, M. (2020). *How much does it cost own a chicken? Egg cost comparison.* The Frugal Chicken. https://thefrugalchicken.com/ how-much-does-it-cost-own-a-chicken/#Feeding_Chickens

Walker, J. (n.d.). *8 different types of chicken feeds.* Coops and Cages. https://www.coopsandcages.com.au/blog/8-different-types-chicken-feeds/

WebMD Editorial Contributors. (2022). *Health benefits of chicken.* WebMD https://www.webmd.com/diet/health-benefits-chicken#:~:text=A%20food%20rich%20in%20pro-tein,the%20risk%20of%20heart%20disease.&text=Chicken%20con-tains%20the%20amino%20acid,%E2%80%9D%20hormone

Wilis, K. (2022). *How much does a chicken coop cost? Get more cluck for your buck.* Angi. https://www.angi.com/articles/how-much-cost-build-chicken-coop.htm

Wilke, L. (n.d.). *Chicken coop design – important features.* Better Hens and Gardens. https://www.betterhensandgardens.com/chicken-coop-designs-10-important-features/#:~:text=The%20important%20housing%20elements%20to,and%20water%20should%20be%20considered

IMAGE REFERENCES

Ovidiu. (n.d.) *Easy chicken coop plans.* Myoutdoorplans. https://myout doorplans.com/animals/easy-chicken-coop-plans/

www.ingramcontent.com/pod-product-compliance
Lightning Source LLC
Chambersburg PA
CBHW021400150726
47989CB00005B/2339